GOD'S LAWS

OF

HEALING

A CHRISTIAN'S GUIDE TO HEALING MIRACLES

FRANCES LANGE

GOD'S LAWS OF HEALING

A CHRISTIAN'S GUIDE TO HEALING MIRACLES

Copyright © 2020 by Frances Lange
ISBN: 978-1-7358149-0-2

Faith Practitioners Publishing
P.O. Box 627
Dickinson, TX 77539

All Scripture quotations in this book are taken from the King James Version of the Bible.

O LORD my God, I cried unto thee,
and thou hast healed me.

—Psalm 30:2

Contents

Introduction

It is important to understand that supernatural healing manifestations are governed by spiritual laws that God has put in place. Everything in God's kingdom, and the spiritual realm in general, operates by the laws of that realm. When you see someone receive a miraculous healing, *there were spiritual laws put to work behind the scenes that caused that event to take place.* If you learn how these laws work, you can "duplicate" the results. This is God's intention, as his desire is for us to live healthily and minister healing to others. Supernatural intervention and miracles are supposed to be evident in the common life of a Christian, and yet many Christians do not even realize this. Healing is a *covenant promise* by God to all his children. God will not (and cannot) break his word.

This book will walk you through the truths of God's word regarding healing, and it will highlight the spiritual laws Jesus taught us throughout his healing ministry so you can receive your healing miracle!

If you have prayed and prayed without results, it is imperative to dig deep into how the laws of healing work. Faith only works to your knowledge level. The word says, "My people are destroyed for lack of knowledge" (Hosea 4:6).

This book will also cover how to apply the knowledge of the laws of healing by showing you how to put those laws into practice to see the miracle manifestation.

Some of you may already have some understanding of these teachings, while others may find it completely foreign. If you want to see God's healing power flow in your life, you must decide to give God's word *first place* in your heart. You must give God's word final authority on the matter, above your own thoughts and opinions. If what you have been taught does not line up with the word of God, discard every belief you have held that has been contrary to his word! Do not *ever* place someone else's opinion or experience (or your own) above the word of God. If it doesn't seem like the word matches the experiences you have had, the disconnect is not on God's end, and God is not a liar!

If you want to see the miraculous, you will have to accept God's word as the ultimate truth and trust him completely, with your whole heart. This is where we experience the realm of miracles!

It is definitely possible to see immediate results as you plant these truths in your heart and pray for your healing. Others may find that they walk out their healing. This book is meant to be used daily as a guide to assist in continually positioning yourself to see the miraculous.

Christians Have Power to Heal

It is our *job* as Christians to heal the sick (including ourselves), raise the dead, cast out devils, etc. *Yes, I said it is our job.* If we do not see these results in our lives, we are missing something in the word. Let's look at what the word says about our power and authority.

"And when he had called unto him his twelve disciples, he gave them power against unclean spirits, to cast them out, and to heal all manner of sickness and all manner of disease" (Matthew 10:1).

❖ We have been given the power necessary. Jesus delegated God's power to Christians, as we clearly see here. It was (and is) God's intent to have Christians minister these miracles and to behave like Jesus (our example).

"And as ye go, preach, saying, The kingdom of heaven is at hand. Heal the sick, cleanse the lepers, raise the dead, cast out devils: freely ye have received, freely give" (Matthew 10:7–8).

❖ Jesus is telling us what to do with the power he gave us.

❖ Healing the sick (along with everything else in this Scripture) is a *command*. When he tells us to do something, it is not optional or a "maybe." He is telling us to do it, period.

❖ *We* heal the sick. Jesus told them flat out to go heal the sick. Let me clarify that a little. Of course it is God who does the miracle (it is by his Spirit that lives in us), and we (by faith) recognize this and allow his power to work through us, but *we heal the sick*!! We don't ask God; he already told us what to do here! We don't have to question if it is his will. Clearly, we don't beg God to do anything. We have a part in ministering healing, and we do it with the power he gave us access to because he commanded us to do it.

❖ Also notice it says, "freely give." This doesn't sound anything like, "Every once in a while, we may see the miracles of God." Healing (and the other things listed) should be a part of our everyday walk as Christians. In addition, God tells *us* to freely give. We couldn't give anything to anyone that we didn't already possess or have the power to give.

"And these signs shall follow them that believe; In my name shall they cast out devils; they shall speak with new tongues; They shall take up serpents; and if they drink any deadly thing, it shall not hurt them; they shall lay hands on the sick, and they shall recover" (Mark 16:17–18).

- ❖ Jesus said the above Scripture after he told his disciples to go into all the world and preach the gospel to every creature. Therefore, "them *that believe*" means *any person* who will believe what Jesus said. It was not just the disciples that would see these miracles in their ministry. It is any Christ follower from then on!

- ❖ "And these signs *shall* follow." What we see from this is that it is not a *maybe*. This is what every Christian (who will believe it) will see in their walk. It is the norm, not the rarity! *It is expected.* On the flip side, we also see from this that if you are a Christian and don't believe these words Jesus spoke, you *will not* have these signs follow you.

- ❖ Another important note we learn from this Scripture is that Christians do not need the special gifts (of faith, miracles, healings, etc.) to do this. While the gifts have their places, if they were necessary to do this in every case, he wouldn't tell us that all these signs shall follow any Christian that believes. Christians don't get to choose which gifts they receive, and though every Christian does receive spiritual gifts, they don't receive all the gifts necessarily. That tells us that you don't need these gifts to see these results, otherwise what Jesus told us we would do would be impossible. There is more than one way to receive healing. That does not negate that gifts are necessary to the purpose of God as a whole, however. Another important thing to remember is that if a situation needs a gift in operation, God can and does cause people to operate in gifts that they don't necessarily operate in regularly. Either way, we need to have faith, step out on the word, and expect to see the power of God work to heal (for ourselves and others). We don't back off from this just because we don't feel we operate in the "gift of healing," as that is not scriptural.

Something we need to address right here at the beginning of this journey is that you must be a Christian to have access to the power of God and to use this authority. Jesus must be your Lord for you to use his name. This is an account of some men who attempted to cast out an evil spirit but were not Christians. They said, "We adjure you by Jesus whom Paul preacheth," and this is what happened: "And the evil spirit answered and said, Jesus I know, and Paul I know; but who are ye? And the man in whom the evil spirit was leaped on them, and overcame them, and prevailed against them, so that they fled out of that house naked and wounded" (Acts 19:15–16).

If you are reading this and you are not a Christian, don't think it is an accident! If you have been asking God to reveal himself to you, *here is your sign*. There are going to be people that read this one paragraph, and you are going to know that God is saying this directly to you and that it is time to accept him as Lord of your life. How do I know this? Because I have been going along writing this book (I would guess I am about halfway through), and the Lord spoke to me and told me to go back to the first chapter and write this. So, *this is for you*.

This is what the Lord is saying to you:

"For God so loved the world, that he gave his only begotten Son, that whosoever believeth in him should not perish, but have everlasting life" (John 3:16).

"Jesus saith unto him, 'I am the way, the truth, and the life: no man cometh unto the Father, but by me'" (John 14:6).

"For whosoever shall call upon the name of the Lord shall be saved" (Romans 10:13).

"For with the heart man believeth unto righteousness; and with the mouth confession is made unto salvation" (Romans 10:10).

God loves you. Yes, *you*. You can't earn salvation; you just receive it. It is time to settle this in your heart. Pray this prayer right now with sincerity:

Jesus, I believe you died on the cross for my sins and that you were raised from the dead. I ask you to come into my heart and be Lord in my life. I repent of my sins, and I receive your forgiveness right now. I come to you just as I am, and I give my life to you. Thank you that you are changing me for your glory. In your name I pray, amen.

That's it! If you prayed that prayer, you are a child of God and a citizen of God's kingdom. Right this minute, you have access to all that God has. And you have access to his healing power. Remember, you don't earn it (you can't). It is a gift from him to you.

Now get ready to see the goodness of God! He is the healer, and he always comes through!

Methods of Healing

There are different ways healing occurs. You may be a Christian seeking the Lord for healing for yourself, or you may be growing in your knowledge of God's word to minister healing to others. It is important to understand the different ways healing manifests.

Natural Healing and Medicine

God designed the body to heal itself naturally. Everyone has experienced this healing process, most likely on several occasions. If you have ever had a cold or an infection of some sort and you recovered from it without a supernatural occurrence, you experienced natural healing. Remember, even natural healing is a gift from God. This also points to the fact that God wants people well, not sick. He designed our bodies to recover from sickness and disease.

When it comes to medicine, in general we as Christians should not be against it. Unless God specifically told you not to take medication or a certain treatment, there is no harm in doing so! If you do not want to take medication or follow a treatment plan advised by your doctor, seek God as to what he has to say about it. God does perform healing through medicine, so we should not become so spiritual that we discount that! While man is the one who has created medicines in the natural, we must remember that every good gift comes from God, and he also is the orchestrator of these discoveries.

Keep in mind that if you have peace about being healed on your faith without natural medicine, that is your choice, and it is between you and God. We do see scriptural evidence that supports that we have some say in *how* we are healed (more on that later).

Supernatural Healing – God's Intervention

While technically the other supernatural healing methods listed in this book are also God intervening, here I am referencing when God steps in and moves at his own desire and discretion for the sake of his purpose. When you are seeking healing for yourself or for someone else, that manifestation will typically fall under the other methods of supernatural healing. While this book will mainly cover those other methods, it is still important to highlight this as one way God's healing manifests to see the difference.

An example of this method is the man in John 5 who the Bible says could not walk and had an infirmity for thirty-eight years. The man would lay by the pool of Bethesda because at a certain season an angel would come and stir the waters, and the first person into the water would receive a healing miracle. Jesus came upon the man there (the man did not seek Jesus out), and he walked up and asked the man, "Wilt thou be made whole?" (verse 6)

The man told Jesus of how others would step out and get into the pool before he was able, and Jesus replied, "Rise, take up thy bed, and walk" (verse 8). The Bible says the man was immediately made whole, and he got up, picked up his bed, and began walking.

I am using this example because it reflects this particular method of healing by showing us that there are healings and other miracles that happen at God's choosing. Again, this man did not seek out Jesus, Jesus just went up to him and healed him. Other methods of supernatural healing show us very clearly that we can put a demand in the spirit to receive healing for ourselves when we desire or on the behalf of others.

Supernatural Healing – The Gift of Healing

This references Christians who operate in a special gift of healing. There are many spiritual gifts; however, they are distributed to believers as the Spirit wills, not based on our desire. I am not going into this method in depth, but it needs to be noted, as it is another method by which people receive their healing miracle. This gift has its place in God's design and purpose. It is mainly to draw people to God and is a tangible display to them of his love, goodness, and power. This gift is also important to the body of Christ because there are many Christians who don't understand their covenant promise of healing and how to receive it on their own faith or how to minister healing to others on their own faith. (If you don't understand how to receive a healing for yourself based on the promises of God by your own faith, you will not be able to minister healing to others based on these spiritual laws either.) The gift of healing (and other spiritual gifts) is a method God uses to bring healing to those who haven't yet spiritually matured to receive healing by other methods. God also uses this gift to display signs and wonders to draw people to him.

Supernatural Healing – for Yourself, by Your Faith

This is God's highest desire for all Christians. He wants all believers to grow in their understanding and relationship with him to receive healing and all the other promises of God. The Bible says that the same Spirit that raised Christ from the dead lives in us. All that power is within us! This book will reveal much around this topic and how to use that power according to God's spiritual laws to manifest healing. It is important to come to this understanding and revelation in our spiritual walk with the Lord. One reason we don't see more of the miracles of God in our lives is due to the lack of knowledge around these truths! We don't need someone with a special anointing. When it comes to our healing, we have a covenant promise, and by God's design, we have the ability to receive anything in the covenant by our faith. You will notice the different accounts of healing in Jesus's ministry where he says things like, "According to your faith, be it unto you," and "Your faith hath made thee whole." In these cases, he is purposely telling us that is how the miracle came to pass. He is teaching us and instructing us so we can receive our healing (or any other miracle needed according to the promises) with our faith.

Supernatural Healing – for Others, by Your Faith

YES, others can be healed on your faith. This seems to be debated somewhat, but the Scriptures are quite clear. There are several examples in the Bible of this, and we will look at them in depth in another chapter. When you pray and believe God for healing for someone else, seeing what the word says regarding it will solidify your faith so you can see the miracle manifest.

This chapter brings light to the different truths found in God's word that govern healing. God's kingdom exists in the spiritual realm, and it is governed by laws. The same way the earth is governed by laws. God does not violate his own laws; this is vital to understand. You have to "position" yourself for a miracle to see the manifestation, and in order to do that, you have to know how these laws operate. That being said, once you've seen something is scriptural regarding God's laws of healing, you can't neglect it and still expect to see good results. He that has an ear, let him hear!

#1 Healing Is Always God's Will.

This is the first thing you must settle in your heart as truth to position yourself for healing or to release your faith for someone else's healing. If you don't believe it is God's will, you will struggle with having faith to receive healing from God. Later in this chapter you will see that Jesus purchased your healing. Jesus would not have endured that part of the atonement if it was not God's will to heal.

"Beloved, I wish above all things that thou mayest prosper and be in health, even as thy soul prospereth" (3 John 1:2).

"The thief cometh not, but for to steal, and to kill, and to destroy: I am come that they might have life, and that they might have it more abundantly" (John 10:10).

"For I am the LORD that healeth thee" (Exodus 15:26).

#2 God's Will Does Not Automatically Come to Pass.

So many people think that if it was God's will to heal, then he would do it. We have already shown with supported Scripture that *we* have the authority and power of God to heal and that he gave us the commandment to do it. It is up to us to agree with and release that power according to his laws of healing to see our healing manifest. Once God establishes a law and covenant, he cannot break it. God is constrained to move according to the partnership he made with us.

The Bible says that God wants all people saved, he doesn't want anyone to perish, and yet people reject Jesus all the time. His will is definitely not coming to pass in every single person's life, but we see that it is at *their* choosing, not God's. Once God has given us the authority and the right to choose him or not, he does not override that authority he gave us to make our own choices. Look at all the evil going on in the world. Do you really think that evil is the will of a good and loving God? NO! God has partnered with us on this earth, and we have a part to play!

#3 God Never Says No to Healing.

Some people think that there are times God does not choose to heal. First of all, God is not making *any* choices regarding healing anymore because *he already made his decision!* If we look at the ministry of Jesus, we find that God *never* said no to healing. Not once. Every person who approached Jesus for healing received it. Also, it is important to note, Jesus never said a sickness was placed on someone by God, or that it was a punishment, or that the person had the sickness to teach them something. That is not scriptural; it is a false doctrine contrary to God's word. The only time Jesus could not heal (and notice that says *could not*, not that he *would not*) was when there was unbelief present in those who lived in his hometown. More information on that account is given later in this book, but the key point under this truth is that God always said yes (and still says yes because his decision was established) to healing for those that were willing to receive.

#4 Healing Was Purchased by Jesus.

Healing was something Jesus *paid* for when he went to the cross. The Bible says that by his stripes, we were healed. God has never done anything for no reason. If Jesus just died for our sins to redeem us so we could be born again and go to heaven, he would not have had to take the stripes on his back.

Back then, this punishment, also referred to as the "forty minus one" lashes, was used and was considered a high form of torture. The Romans had determined that they could sentence someone to thirty-nine lashes without actually killing the person. This was a *brutal* punishment. God was purposeful in allowing this punishment to be placed on Jesus. Scripture clearly tells us he endured the lashings to purchase our healing! He bore our sicknesses so we could be healed! Again, he did not have to do this if all he intended to do was provide redemption for us. If that were the case, all he had to do was give his life for ours.

It is important that we do not take for granted and brush over all that Jesus endured on our behalf. It is an *actual insult* to all that God offered us as a gift, which we could never earn. (That is why your healing is not promised based on who you are or how perfect you are, it is based on what Jesus did for you.) Jesus cried, "It is finished," when he accomplished all that he was sent to do at the cross. Your healing was purchased right then along with your salvation. Your healing is a *covenant promise,* and it has already been granted!

"But he was wounded for our transgressions, he was bruised for our iniquities: the chastisement of our peace was upon him; and with his stripes we are healed" (Isaiah 53:5).

"Himself took our infirmities, and bare our sicknesses" (Matthew 8:17).

#5 God Is Not the Author of Sickness.

This truth is easy to see when we look at what Jesus said. We cannot blame God, thinking he is the one who made us sick! We go to God to receive healing!

"The thief cometh not, but for to steal, and to kill, and to destroy: I am come that they might have life, and that they might have it more abundantly" (John 10:10).

#6 God Is Bound by His Word to Heal.

If God promised healing as part of his covenant with us, he is bound by his word to bring it to pass! When someone does not receive healing, the disconnect is *never* on God's end. Remember, it is always God's will to heal: Jesus purchased your healing by the stripes he took on his back. Healing is made available to every person who wants to receive it. Period. There are other reasons why people don't receive the healing miracle that God has already made available for the taking, but it has nothing to do with God. Sometimes people don't receive because of their lack of knowledge of the laws that govern healing. There are also things that can block the healing from manifesting (more on this later). The bottom line is that God is bound by his word, he does not "take it back," and he cannot lie!

"God is not a man, that he should lie; neither the son of man, that he should repent: hath he said, and shall he not do it? or hath he spoken, and shall he not make it good?" (Numbers 23:19)

"My covenant will I not break, nor alter the thing that is gone out of my lips" (Psalm 89:34).

#7 God Will Reveal to You How Healing "Works."

God is not trying to hide how healing miracles manifest from us. Sometimes people think they are slaving away, praying, and trying to do the right things and say the right things to get God to move or reveal things to them. That is an improper view of our heavenly Father. He wants us to have this knowledge and receive healing even more that we do! As you study healing and step out in faith, God will reveal to you everything you need to know. Have confidence in the goodness of God to be faithful to his word!

"If any of you lack wisdom, let him ask of God, that giveth to all men liberally, and upbraideth not; and it shall be given him" (James 1:5).

"For every one that asketh receiveth; and he that seeketh findeth; and to him that knocketh it shall be opened" (Matthew 7:8).

#8 All Christians Have the Power to Heal.

We have gone over this truth in the first chapter. Any Christian who will believe the word of God and step out in faith can see healing manifest for themselves and for others. God does not pick and choose, and as already stated, Jesus commanded us to go out and heal the sick. When he was teaching his disciples, he was showing them how to continue his ministry and how to train other Christians to do the same.

#9 You Don't Need a Gift of Healing to Heal.

We also referenced this in the first chapter. If the only way to see healing miracles was through a gift of healing, then Jesus would not have commanded all believers to go out and preach the gospel to every creature and to heal the sick. The gift of healing is used to accomplish God's will in certain circumstances and is not necessary to fulfill a Christian's everyday walk of ministering healing to themselves and others.

#10 The Healing Power Is IN You.

Healing miracles manifest from within you. The Bible says the same Spirit that raised Christ from the dead dwells *in* you. You are not reaching out somewhere else to get your miracle; you are positioning yourself to receive by his Spirit that is in you. (And the healing is *already* accomplished in the Spirit.)

#11 Performing Healing Miracles Is a Commandment.

This was also discussed in the first chapter where we covered our power and authority as Christians to heal. Seeing healing as a command builds our faith, because when we realize this truth, it snuffs out doubts as to whether it is God's will to heal, and it gives us confidence that we have the power and authority to heal. God wouldn't command us to do anything he didn't authorize or grant us the power to do!

#12 Healing Is Not Earned by How "Good" You Are.

You can't earn healing, salvation, or anything else. If that were the case, Jesus would not have had to die for our sins to redeem us, nor would he have had to suffer the torment when he took the stripes on his back for our healing. God made the covenant he did with us because he knew we could never earn it, because we would never be good enough. Anytime you hear the voice of condemnation, that is not from God (God convicts us, he doesn't condemn us). It actually pleases God when we accept what he did based on how good and faithful he is as a father. When we don't, we are in pride, thinking that any of what we receive from him is based on our own good works.

#13 You Decide If You Get Healed, Not God.

This is profound, and yet many people don't believe this! So many people think it is up to God who gets healed, and they don't realize that if they want to be healed, they can be. Period. If you search the different cases of healing during the ministry of Jesus, many are based on the person's desire to be healed and them seeking out Jesus for healing. And they received their miracle, *every single time.* There were many more miracles performed by Jesus than what has been recorded, but God included what was necessary for us to learn and to answer the questions we would have. He is faithful! God is showing us in these accounts of others that we can expect to be healed if we want to be, we aren't waiting on him to decide. *He already decided* when Jesus purchased our healing and made it available to whosoever will reach out in faith and receive it.

The woman with the issue of blood found in Luke 8 is a prime example of this. Jesus did not speak to her, he didn't seek her out, she didn't even ask him to heal her. The Bible says the woman said to herself that if she could just touch the hem of his garment, she would be made whole. Then she came in the crowd behind Jesus, and when she touched his garment, the Scripture says "and immediately her issue of blood stanched" (verse 44). Then it says Jesus perceived that virtue (power) had gone out of him and asked who had touched him. When she revealed herself and told him what had happened, he said, "Daughter, be of good comfort: thy faith hath made thee whole; go in peace" (verse 48).

This shows very clearly that God has already made healing available to anyone who desires it. Again, the woman decided to be healed and went after her healing, and then she received just as she had believed she would receive it. It wasn't "granted" by God, it was taken by her. It wasn't based on how good of a person she was. Jesus clearly stated she got it because she had faith, and that was all it took.

#14 You Have a Say in How You Are Healed.

This is an interesting point that we see in Scripture, and it is worth noting because it is beyond what many of us think we are "allowed" to expect or pray for. Later in this book we will show the different accounts of healings performed by Jesus along with commentary notes for teaching. In that chapter, you will see it noted when this situation occurred. I will use the example of the woman with the issue of blood here again very quickly to give you more of an idea of what this is referring to. Basically, the woman said to herself that if she could just touch the hem of Jesus's garment, she would be made whole. Then, when she did what she said and had faith for, she received the healing in *that way*. Every single instance where someone made a faith declaration in relation to *how* the healing would manifest, it manifested that way. This gives us scriptural reason to believe we can expect the same thing! If we can have faith for something specifically, we can have it because God is no respecter of persons and the laws of healing worked for others who did the same thing.

#15 Healing Manifests by Your Faith.

This is *huge* when it comes to seeing a miracle! Faith is an absolute requirement, and it is the "vehicle" of miracle manifestation. Let's look at Mark 11:22–24:

And Jesus answering saith unto them, Have faith in God. For verily I say unto you, That whosoever shall say unto this mountain, Be thou removed, and be thou cast into the sea; and shall not doubt in his heart, but shall believe that those things which he saith shall come to pass; he shall have whatsoever he saith. Therefore I say unto you, What things soever ye desire, when ye pray, believe that ye receive them, and ye shall have them.

This is Jesus teaching us how miracles happen and showing us that they are *directly dependent* on our faith. Many people don't fully understand what faith is, and oftentimes they don't realize that they are not really in faith. This alone is a common reason people do not see their healing manifest. We will discuss faith and its operation in greater depth in another chapter, as getting a hold of this law is paramount to receiving healing.

#16 Faith Comes by Hearing.

This is how you position yourself to receive your healing. In the spiritual realm, this is how things operate, so it is of the utmost importance to understand this law! If you look at the ministry of Jesus, he went about preaching the gospel before he performed miracles during his teachings. There is a reason for this:

the word of God prepares and causes the *spirit* to receive spiritual things (by igniting faith). Physical strength comes by physical exercise. Your physical body needs food and water to survive and to be nourished. Hearing the word of God is what affects and feeds the spirit!

You cannot neglect this law and use your faith to receive miracles. You also cannot spend time building your faith for something for a week and then stop. It works the same way as your physical body does. You must *continually* feed your body, thus you must continually feed your spirit. There is supernatural power in the word of God: it becomes alive to you, and new revelations come as you constantly plant the word in your spirit (heart). As a result, faith comes.

"So then faith cometh by hearing, and hearing by the word of God" (Romans 10:17).

Another thing we learn from this law is how unbelief and other things that are contrary to the character of God get into our being. This law is showing us how things work in the spiritual realm. Things other than faith get into our heart the same way faith does! We plant beliefs and thoughts into our spirit by feeding on them. Our spirit is exposed to what we hear, see, meditate and think on, etc. Not only do we need to proactively and intentionally feed on and put God's word *in*, we also must be on guard and keep everything contrary to what he says *out!*

An example would be to begin to feed your spirit by reading all the Scriptures and accounts regarding healing in the Bible, listening to teachings on healing, etc. Now, not only do you feed your spirit those things, but you *must also fast from* (avoid putting in) everything that speaks death and disease. Don't constantly be reading online all the negative things about your illness (this does not mean don't be educated, but at some point, take your focus off this, and do it quickly). Don't speak to your friends and family about how sick you are and all the doom and gloom. Begin to combat all the negative thoughts you have been allowing to roll over and over in your mind (this is a form of meditating on the sickness instead of on God's healing promises). Replace those thoughts with God's promises, and begin declaring them.

#17 Faith Doesn't Work without Love.

This is also key. God *is* love. We need to be constantly checking our love walk. If you want your faith to work, you must walk in love. Miracles don't work without faith, and faith doesn't work without love. If you are constantly angry with people, being ugly, gossiping, etc., don't expect to see miracles manifest. One thing I have noticed the enemy do when I am believing God for serious miracles is try to get me into strife with someone. It is not worth it! Be on guard with your heart! This is a way the enemy actually *paralyzes* your faith.

"But faith which worketh by love" (Galatians 5:6).

"And though I have the gift of prophecy, and understand all mysteries, and all knowledge; and though I have all faith, so that I could remove mountains, and have not charity, I am nothing" (1 Corinthians 13:2). ("Charity" here is love.)

#18 Faith Must Have Corresponding Works.

This does not mean we actually work to perform the miracle. God's Spirit that lives within us does the work.

"Believest thou not that I am in the Father, and the Father in me? the words that I speak unto you I speak not of myself: but the Father that dwelleth in me, he doeth the works" (John 14:10).

Nor does "works" here mean we work to earn anything, as already mentioned earlier (he does the work). This just means we walk, talk, act, and think in faith. If there is no corresponding action to your faith, it does nothing.

"Even so faith, if it hath not works, is dead, being alone" (James 2:17).

Examples of corresponding "works" would be that we speak the word of God and declare his promises. We make decisions based on the expected outcome of God's word, regardless of what the situation looks like in the natural. We have a thankful and a rejoicing heart and attitude as though the manifestation has already taken place. A more specific example would be that if you are believing God for a new house, you begin designing the house and taking the steps to prepare for it! If you believe you receive the miracle when you pray, then all your actions, words, thoughts, and attitude surrounding that reflect it! You act like you believe God.

#19 Your Words Establish the Miracle or Kill It.

Make no mistake, the words you say matter, and they matter a lot. Some people think that this concept is a bunch of hocus-pocus, but there are so many Scriptures in the Bible that show this is true. God used words to speak the world into existence. Faith is released with our words. In order to manifest your healing, you must *speak* to the mountain! Likewise, you also must *refrain from speaking* things contrary to God's promises regarding your healing! In Mark 11, Jesus said to *speak* to your mountain and command it to be removed. This is all throughout the Bible, but let's just look at that account again for now. Pay attention to how many times Jesus noted how important speaking is in relation to manifesting the miracle.

> For verily I say unto you, That whosoever shall *say* unto this mountain, Be thou removed, and be thou cast into the sea; and shall not doubt in his heart, but shall believe that those things which he *saith* shall come to pass; he shall have whatsoever he *saith*. Therefore I say unto you, What things soever ye desire, when ye pray, believe that ye receive them, and ye shall have them. (Mark 11:23–24, emphasis added)

"Death and life are in the power of the tongue" (Proverbs 18:21).

"Thou shalt also decree a thing, and it shall be established unto thee" (Job 22:28).

#20 You Must Ignore the Contrary Circumstances.

The word teaches us that we are to totally ignore every circumstance that says anything other than that we are healed. This concept was also touched on under the law Faith Comes by Hearing above, but I want to clearly depict this element separately.

Why is it important to ignore these things and not give them any attention with our minds and hearts? Because they bring unbelief into us and make us doubt. In the account of Peter walking on the water, while it wasn't a healing miracle, it is important because it shows us how unbelief will get in and stop miracles from manifesting. This is true for any miracle we need, including healing.

When Peter stepped out on the water to go to Jesus (who was already walking on the water), he started to walk on the water. However, when he saw the boisterous wind, he became afraid and then began to sink. Jesus caught him and said, "O thou of little faith, wherefore didst thou doubt?" (Matthew 14:31). It wasn't looking at the circumstances that stopped the miracle, it was because looking at those circumstances caused doubt and unbelief, and unbelief blocks miracles. We will go more into this account next.

#21 Unbelief Blocks Miracles.

In the Scriptures found in Mark 11 noted in previous paragraphs, if you read that again you will see where it tells you that if you *don't doubt in your heart*, but believe those things that you say will come to pass, you will have them. Jesus made a point to tell us that we must believe, but he also made a point to tell us not to have *unbelief* when he said not to doubt in our hearts.

In the account of the epileptic boy in Matthew 17, the boy's father brought him to the disciples, but they could not cast out the demon causing the sickness. After Jesus cast the demon out and cured the boy, the disciples asked him why they couldn't cast him out:

And Jesus said unto them, Because of your unbelief: for verily, I say unto you, If ye have faith as a grain of mustard seed, ye shall say unto this mountain, Remove hence to yonder place; and it shall remove; and nothing shall be impossible unto you (Matthew 17:20).

Jesus still pointed to the fact that you need faith for the mountain to move, but the disciples had faith, as they had already performed miracles, and that was why they were stumped when it didn't work that time. Jesus had to clarify further that while you need faith to manifest miracles, it is also important to not be in unbelief, and their unbelief was the very thing that stopped them from seeing the manifestation. With that being said, let's look at what else Jesus told the disciples regarding dealing with this type of unbelief, as it tells us something about an upcoming law we will look at regarding fasting. This Scripture follows right after Jesus told the disciples that their unbelief was the issue: "Howbeit this kind goeth not out but by prayer and fasting" (Matthew 17:21).

It is important to understand that Jesus was talking about unbelief when he said "this kind." He was not talking about a demon, as many have interpreted. So, we see the issue of unbelief blocking the miracle, and the need for fasting to rectify it in this case. This also shows us that there are different kinds of unbelief, and some unbelief requires fasting to overcome.

#22 Unforgiveness Blocks Miracles.

This goes hand in hand with walking in love and the previous notation that faith *works* by love. Again, you will not see miracles manifest if you don't walk in love and you hold on to unforgiveness. We have already looked at the Scriptures in Mark 11 where Jesus taught the disciples how miracles manifest when he talked to them about speaking to the mountain and commanding it to be removed, not doubting in their hearts, having faith, and believing that what they said would come to pass. He told them that if they believed they received the miracle when they prayed, they would then see it manifest in the natural. *Right after* Jesus said that in Mark, he said this: "And when ye stand praying, forgive, if ye have ought against any: that your Father also which is in heaven may forgive you your trespasses" (Mark 11:25).

There is a *reason* Jesus said this about forgiveness directly following his teaching on manifesting miracles, and that is because unforgiveness blocks the power of God from flowing through you! If you are holding on to unforgiveness, you don't have to *feel* like forgiving the person. Feelings have nothing to do with it! All you have to do is make a choice to forgive and release them, stop rehearsing the infraction, and pray for them. When you do this, your feelings will eventually catch up!

#23 You Reap What You Sow.

This a real verse in the Bible, not just a saying. When we hear this, many times we think of it in terms of being nice to people. Such as, don't do to someone what you wouldn't want them doing to you, don't be lazy or you won't get a good return on what you are working for, etc.

While all that is true, there is much more to look at regarding this law and how it affects miracle manifestation. We have already looked at the law regarding how faith comes, this just takes that further and builds on it. What are you sowing? Are your thoughts, words, and actions telling a story of defeat and sickness, or are they telling the story of your healing miracle? Whatever you are sowing into yourself in these different ways is what you will have (reap). That is what this spiritual law is telling us. Now, look at everything you give attention to, and ask yourself, Does this sow faith or unbelief?

When it comes to sickness, many times we have difficult symptoms. Those symptoms sow unbelief. They are sending a message through your physical senses to your mind that tells you that you are sick. During these times, it is even *more important* to sow God's truth into your spirit to combat and get your focus off the temporary facts you are experiencing. Miracles don't come by agreeing with your current situation, they come by calling those things that are not as though they are! (Romans 4:17)

#24 Some Sickness Requires Casting Out Demons.

This makes some people uncomfortable, but it is reality. There is no reason to be afraid of demons, the power we have in Christ is greater than anything.

"Ye are of God, little children, and have overcome them: because greater is he that is in you, than he that is in the world" (1 John 4:4).

There were accounts during Jesus's ministry where he had to cast out the demons to set the person free and for the healing to come. The demon was the cause of the physical ailment in these cases. You can find these accounts in the case studies included at the end of this book, but here are a few examples:

- ❖ The woman who was bent over and could not lift herself up in Luke 13:11–13.
- ❖ The epileptic boy that the disciples couldn't cure because of their unbelief in Matthew 17:14–21.
- ❖ The blind and dumb (mute) man in Matthew 12:22 and Luke 11:14.
- ❖ The dumb (mute) man in Matthew 9:32–33.

There are also several accounts of multitudes of people being healed, and the Bible tells us that Jesus healed all types of diseases and cast out devils. In those accounts it doesn't tell us about the specific situations of the people, so we don't know if there were cases where people had to have devils cast out to cure their physical ailments, or if it is just telling us that both issues were dealt with. However, other accounts show us that people absolutely can and are afflicted physically by demons, and in those cases the demons had to be cast out.

Do not ignore this, and don't be afraid of it. Again, the word is here to teach us, and these accounts are included in what was recorded for us. God's purpose in doing that was so that we would know that these are situations we will encounter so we will deal with them properly. We will go more in depth on this topic in another chapter.

#25 Fasting Is a Requirement for Some Miracles.

When we are standing for a miracle, it is quite clear, according to the notes and Scriptures shown previously, that there are certain circumstances where we can't position ourselves to receive the manifestation without fasting. This has nothing to do with "works" as though fasting is some sort of penance we pay. What fasting does is show our commitment to God and our desire to push past our fleshly desires and focus on our relationship with God and learning from him. It is designed to bring us into closer intimacy with him and causes spiritual growth and strength when our spirit dominates over our flesh. It is during these times that we receive great revelation from God and experience his presence in a different way, which elevates our faith and starves our unbelief.

It would be good to remember the epileptic boy and how the disciples could not cure him and reflect again on the fact that the disciples had already performed other miracles! Imagine that was you. If you have not seen actual miracles come to pass to date, you may be tempted to think that if you did you would not be in unbelief. However, even with the experiences the disciples already had, there were still circumstances when the miracle that was needed required fasting to deal with the unbelief to see the manifestation. Don't miss this teaching moment! This is a spiritual key showing us that we need to be fasting in our walk with the Lord, and it has an impact on the miracles we will see!

#26 Violating Natural Healing Laws Blocks Miracles.

Some sickness is there simply because we are violating the natural laws of healing, and correcting that would bring natural healing to the body. That is what needs to be done in those cases. Furthermore, violating natural healing laws could allow sickness that might not be reversed naturally without supernatural intervention. An example would be lung cancer that was most likely the result of smoking. Correcting the issue by quitting smoking at that point will not do away with the cancer on its own. God will heal us when we have made these mistakes and even when they have been willful choices to violate the natural laws if we will get our hearts right before him so we can receive. In another chapter we will discuss this more in depth. In certain circumstances, this area can be an open door that blocks healing if not dealt with.

#27 Sin and Disobedience Block Miracles.

This is a really tough one that can be misunderstood. We already said in another point that you cannot earn your healing and that it is promised to every Christian. That is the truth. If that is the truth, and we don't earn our healing by works, how does sin still play a role?

To summarize this quickly, you can and will receive healing even if you struggle with sin in your life. We are under grace and not under the law. You do not want to get confused in this area because Satan will come and try to accuse you of all of your sins and struggles and tell you that you won't be healed, which is a flat-out lie.

How sin can affect our spiritual walk and the power of God flowing through us has everything to do with the condition of the heart and not the actions themselves. We will cover this more in the chapter detailing blocks to healing.

How Healing Miracles Happen

We've already said that healing miracles manifest according to the laws that govern healing, and we have looked at those laws and methods in summary. I want to be careful here because there isn't a legalistic formula that will make a miracle happen for you. With that being said, there is a pretty good outline in the word that shows us the components of a miracle. We must believe that God is wanting us to understand these things to see miracles. After all, he commanded us to go out and heal the sick (including ourselves), and healing was one of the main components of Jesus's ministry. Healing is always part of it, *he wants us to "get" it.*

How the Healing Miracle Happens Is Actually Quite Simple.

When I say that, I mean the progression of a miracle God has shown us in Scripture is not complicated. It is when we look at each component in depth that we begin to see where we trip up. In this chapter, we are going to look at the outline of *how* miracles happen. The rest of this book will help you fully understand each aspect in more depth and provides tools to help you receive your healing manifestation.

The Progression of Miracle Manifestation

The miracle progression diagram on the next page is a tool to see how the healing power of God flows from the Spirit that lives in you to manifestation in your physical body. The manifestation must move from the spiritual realm (top of diagram) to the natural realm (bottom of diagram). You can see from the diagram that faith is the *vehicle* that allows the *movement* from one realm to the other.

The only way to be in faith is by hearing the word of God, and you must continually hear. You can't stop feeding faith in and live on your faith from last month, it doesn't work that way. While faith is the vehicle (so you must have faith), the fuel source to cause faith to "move" things from one realm to the other includes the items listed. From this diagram, you can also see that there are opposing forces to faith that stop your faith from working and stop the miracle from moving from the spiritual realm into the natural. *It is not enough* just to have faith and focus on the things that fuel faith. You must also remove the forces that work in the opposite direction that are bringing resistance to your faith.

While the diagram provides a good snapshot of how miracles happen, you need to *fully understand* each component of God's laws and the things that hinder miracles in order to *implement* that knowledge in your life and act on it to see the healing manifest.

HEALING MIRACLE
Spiritual Realm

You move what is in your spirit to your physical body. You do that by faith.

To <u>Move</u>, Faith Needs
- Right Belief/God's Laws
- Works by Love
- Corresponding Actions
- Released by Words

To <u>Be in</u> Faith
Faith comes by hearing. You must *continue hearing* to be in faith.

FAITH ALLOWS MOVEMENT

OPPOSING FORCES
(Blocks Manifestation = Backward Movement)

Opposing forces will block your faith from moving and move you away from miracle manifestation. *Fasting required in some cases.

Stop/Remove Opposition
- Unbelief
- Unforgiveness
- Disobedience/Sin
- Spirit of Infirmity
- Violating Natural Laws

HEALING MANIFESTATION
Physical Realm

The Components of Miracle Manifestation

The progression diagram showing how a miracle flows from the spiritual realm to the natural helps us see how a miracle works *in action*. Now we will look at each of those components in more detail. The laws of healing outlined earlier in the book all fit into three different categories of the process:

1) Put the right things in your heart (spirit).
2) Act on your faith.
3) Keep the wrong things out of your heart (spirit).

The first two categories are what you do to receive your healing (also depicted on the progression diagram). Putting the right things in your heart and acting on your faith is what causes the movement to bring what is in the spiritual realm into the physical realm. The third category includes the things that block you from receiving (also depicted on the progression diagram). *If you aren't doing the first two things, there is nothing to block because you aren't receiving to begin with. Likewise, if you are doing the first two things, but not removing the blocks, your faith goes nowhere and/or is hindered.*

Summary of Miracle Components

Here is a look at the miracle components on the progression diagram in list form.

Miracle Component	What It Does
1) Knowledge/Right Beliefs • The first step to a miracle is knowing and believing God's laws about healing. • Must have proper faith foundation. (This determines *what* you have faith for.)	Shapes Faith (*What* you believe defines the miracle you receive.)
2) Be in Faith • Faith is the vehicle of miracles. • Faith comes by hearing and meditating on God's word continually.	Moves miracle from spiritual realm to physical realm.
3) Walk in Love • Faith works by love. If you don't walk in love, your faith won't do anything. (It will not produce healing.)	Fuels Faith
4) Works Required (Faith Actions) • Faith without works is dead. If your faith doesn't have corresponding actions, it will not produce healing.	Fuels Faith

5) Remove Unforgiveness • Forgiveness is required, it is not an option.	Blocks Miracle
6) Remove Unbelief • Miracles don't happen if you allow unbelief to stay.	Blocks Miracle
7) Remove Sin/Disobedience • Unrepented sin and disobedience are also blocks.	Blocks Miracle
8) Stop Violating Natural Laws • Violating the natural laws of health allows sickness.	Blocks Miracle

Items one through four are the things that we need to be doing (*putting in* the soil of our heart and taking action). The remaining items listed are what we need to be avoiding (*keeping out* of the soil of our heart).

We have already covered these components in summary when we read about God's laws of healing. As we go forward, we will go into depth about faith with examples of what faith is and what it is not. We will also discuss the blocks to healing in more detail, but before we get into that, let's recap why it is so important to have right beliefs and proper knowledge of God's word (#1 on the list).

You need to know what God's word says about healing and have the right belief in your heart regarding God's word because you can't have faith for something if you don't know what God's word says about it. You would be in confusion and doubt (or flat-out believing a lie), which will shape your faith and *define (determine) what you receive.* A simple example of this would be someone who has the belief that when they pray, they may get healed, or they may not because it is not always God's will to heal.

That is a lie, it is a lack of knowledge, and it is not a revelation of the truth. If a person believes this, when they get into the next step of the process, it won't work! You can't have faith to receive something if you don't believe it! If you don't believe it is always God's will to heal and that he already provided healing for you in Jesus, then you won't have faith that you absolutely will be healed. If you don't have faith that you absolutely will be healed, you won't be healed. Do you see how imperative this is to the process? It affects everything else!

I already stated that how the healing miracle happens is quite simple. This is one example that shows why people miss it even though the process itself is not difficult to understand.

A false doctrine will cause you to believe something that is a lie, and you will not receive your miracle. You must take the time to study God's word and the information in this book and others like it. You must first correct each belief you have about healing so that it lines up with God's word before you move on to the

begging God, you aren't using the spiritual law of faith correctly. Some may say he was able to do that because he was Jesus, but Jesus explicitly stated later in the chapter what we are able to do and did not instruct us to ask God to do anything. (Jesus was using the power of God in him, and he was telling us to do the same thing.) Remember, this is a spiritual law, and healing has already been granted, and that is why we don't ask God to do it again.

❖ Jesus *spoke* what he wanted to happen, and he instructed them to do the same. Read it again and notice where Jesus said the words "say" and "saith." Faith is released when you speak the command that lines up with the word of God. It is not released just by reading it or thinking about it.

❖ The *first thing* Jesus told his disciples to do was "Have faith in God." So, you don't just speak words: they must be released with faith. The expectancy you have from your faith is in God's integrity and ability to perform his word.

❖ The *second thing* Jesus told them was "for verily," which means "for *certainly.*" Jesus himself (God in the flesh who cannot lie) was saying, "What I am about to tell   you is *certain.*"

❖ The *third thing* Jesus pointed out was "whosoever." He was saying *anyone* who will take heed to what he was saying and act on it can do it. This totally refutes arguments that only certain people have the ability to do these things.

❖ Then we are back to faith again: "shall not doubt in his heart, but shall believe that those things which he saith." Doubt is *disbelief,* and to believe equals faith.

❖ Finally, in the last statement Jesus made, he said "when ye pray, believe that ye receive." Jesus was saying that that is the moment when faith is released. You believe it is already so (received) when you pray, before you ever actually see it come to pass. That is key! It *is not* faith if you must see it to believe it. And faith is what is necessary to see miracles and impact the natural realm through the spiritual realm. The only way you will ever see these things is if you will get into that place.

So, you start with having faith in God (his integrity and ability), and then you speak to your mountain. We are talking about healing, so you would give the command to your sickness and say something like this: "Cancer I take authority over you in the name of Jesus. By his stripes I was healed, and I command you to go from my body right now. Body, I command you to respond to the word of God and be whole in Jesus's name."

The point is that you command those things, according to what the word says, in faith. And you don't beg! You wouldn't be begging if you had faith. Faith is belief that it is so, and you are certain you will see it manifest in your life. If you are begging, you have already moved out of the spiritual law of faith that holds the supernatural power to see it come to pass.

Faith Is the Vehicle

There are many examples all throughout the Bible that tell us this supernatural force called faith is the vehicle for miracles. It is important to settle this fact in your heart to be able to operate in these things! Here are a few more instances (again this is all throughout the word) showing us that faith is the vehicle and a key that unlocks the door to miracles:

"Then touched he their eyes, saying, According to your faith be it unto you" (Matthew 9:29).

"And he said unto her, Daughter, thy faith hath made thee whole; go in peace, and be whole of thy plague" (Mark 5:34).

"And Jesus said unto him, Go thy way; thy faith hath made thee whole. And immediately he received his sight, and followed Jesus in the way" (Mark 10:52).

"And Jesus said unto the centurion, Go thy way; and as thou hast believed, so be it done unto thee. And his servant was healed in the selfsame hour" (Matthew 8:13).

Reading these Scriptures, it is clear by the words of Jesus himself that faith is a key player in people receiving their miracles. Also notice how he made a point to *tell people why* they were healed (because of their faith). He did that on purpose because he wanted us to be able to understand these things. It is not something God is trying to keep hidden from us!

How to Be in Faith

Maybe you are struggling with this and saying to yourself, "If you have to be in faith when you pray to receive healing, and you have to believe it is done and that you are healed when you pray, but you *don't* believe it even though you try, what do you do?!"

Perhaps what you are believing for is pretty high on the impossible scale, or you just aren't exercised in using your faith. Here is the thing: *you can't* make yourself believe. You choose with your will to believe

God and that God's word is 100% truth and the ultimate authority. Then the supernatural faith (true belief) comes into your heart like this: "So then faith cometh by hearing, and hearing by the word of God" (Romans 10:17).

What does this mean? It means how easy it is for you to be in faith is *directly linked* to how much of God's word you immerse yourself in (and how much you practice it). Word immersion can be many different things: reading the word, listening to sermons, having talks with others about the power of God that builds you up, and praying in tongues, which also builds you up. It is the *power* in the *word* that will then ignite faith (belief) in your heart. You can't make faith come, but if you take the actions that God told you would bring it, those actions will cause faith to rise up in your heart. You can't (in your natural ability) hear you have terminal cancer and then believe, being fully persuaded without doubt, that you will be healed, especially when the doctors have said there is no hope or very little hope. You need supernatural faith in your heart to do that.

If you desperately want to learn how to be effective but you struggle with faith, all you have to do is start immersing yourself in the word. It is not impossible! That is the answer, and it will solve the problem.

Knowing the Word

Since we now know that having the faith you need is dependent on consumption (if you will) of the word, then it becomes clear that knowing the word is also key when it comes to miracle manifestation. If you don't know what the word says about whatever it is you are believing for, then you will not have the faith necessary to receive it, and you won't know if you are submitting to God (within his will) when you are doing these things. We have explained this earlier in the book, regarding having the correct knowledge and belief of God's laws of healing.

Use the healing Scriptures that are included in this book, begin to meditate on God's word, and watch faith come for healing. Speak them out loud and command your body to line up with the word of God in the name of Jesus.

The more you practice, the more natural it will become and the more the word will come alive to you and bring revelation. Some people may hear this and thinks it's crazy or "out there." To those, I would say, Study the word for yourself, you will be amazed at what happens. This, along with other faith builders and exercises, is listed in the Healing Prescription chapter to help you get an action plan together to build your faith and see your healing miracle manifest. This is what the Bible tells us about the word itself:

"For the word of God is quick, and powerful, and sharper than any twoedged sword, piercing even to the dividing asunder of soul and spirit, and of the joints and marrow, and is a discerner of the thoughts and intents of the heart" (Hebrews 4:12).

"Then said the LORD unto me, Thou hast well seen: for I will hasten my word to perform it" (Jeremiah 1:12).

"My son, attend to my words; incline thine ear unto my sayings. Let them not depart from thine eyes; keep them in the midst of thine heart. For they are life unto those that find them, and health to all their flesh" (Proverbs 4:20–22).

Notice here that God is giving you a spiritual truth nugget. The reality is that the word of God is supernatural. This shouldn't be spooky or weird. The laws (how things work) in the physical realm and the spiritual realm are simply different, and the concept is harder to grasp until you begin to study those differences. In the natural, a prime example would be to take medicine (a tangible thing) for a sickness. *God is saying his word is health to our flesh.* (The word "health" in this Scripture is actually the same as the word "medicine.") We may ask ourselves, How can this be? Well, that is probably over all our heads, but just because we don't fully understand the possibility of something does not mean it isn't true.

Get into the word and start practicing your faith! We are to learn to practice these things and implement them in the natural realm the way a doctor practices medicine! It is an amazing thing to team up with God to see his miracles here on earth in our lives and in the lives of those we love. Don't just limit it to your healing, practice your faith even in the small things. God cares about *everything* concerning us. To think we are "bothering" God about the little things is ridiculous, let's not insult his power and ability. He is more than able to handle anything and everything we bring to him. God is not pressed for time in that the little things have to "get in line." The notion of that is hilarious really.

It's time to begin to release your faith on a daily basis for your healing and everything else concerning you! *Practice perfects.*

What Faith Looks Like

We have learned the importance of faith in relation to healing and receiving from God, but what does faith look like in everyday application? I remember when I first started becoming aware of this and noticing the change in my mindset when shifting over into the faith gear. It was definitely one of those "aha" moments for me. All this time I had heard preachers talk about faith and how everything in the spiritual realm is "by faith."

I had faith in God, I believed God's word was true when I heard it, but I had no idea *practically* what it meant to walk by faith (to put it in action). Sometimes it's easier to see what the correct thing is when you understand what the incorrect thing is (where you are in error). Let's look at some examples so we can see more clearly when we are in faith, and when we are not in faith.

Example:

A woman goes to the doctor for the results of further testing she's had done after finding out she has cancer. The doctor gives her a report that she has maybe six months to live, and it is highly unlikely any treatment will make a difference.

Reaction (Not in Faith):

The woman begins to call family and close friends and proceeds to tell them she is dying, that there is nothing the doctors can do for her. She goes on crying and is beside herself and begins rattling off all kinds of things in fear, such as, "What am I going to do? What will my family do without me? What if I am in a lot of pain? What if I don't even live six months? How could God allow this to happen? This is it; this is the end! Even the doctors can't help me, no one can help me, there is no hope!"

We can clearly see from this reaction that there is absolutely nothing being done or said that will manifest healing, and the response is completely outside of the laws of healing. In fact, all it does is release death and agrees with (puts faith in) the doctor's report and not God's report. Now, if you have responded this way regarding whatever ailment you have been dealing with, I have good news! You can disagree with everything you have ever done or said that is contrary to God's word (that says you are healed), break the power of that curse you have released over yourself, and receive God's healing by positioning yourself in line with his word and laws of healing!

Reaction (in Faith):

The woman gets alone before the Lord and prays, saying things along the lines of, "Father you know this is a death sentence the doctors have given me, but I believe you are greater than cancer and any other disease I could ever face. I thank you that you are the Great Physician; that your word says you already purchased my healing; and that by the stripes Jesus took on his back, I am healed. I receive your word, and I am already healed right now. No matter what the doctors or anyone else says, no matter what it looks like or how I feel, I am healed. I walk by faith and not by sight. Be it unto me, according to your word." Then the woman calls family and close friends and gives them the update of what the doctor has said. She tells them (even if through tears) of the prognosis, but then proceeds to tell them that she has already prayed and that she is believing God's word that she is healed. She may ask them (if they are Christians who understand faith) to be in agreement with her regarding her healing and to pray with her.

Walking through the Valley of Sickness (Not in Faith):

Four weeks later the woman has not seen her healing manifest and is starting to experience worse symptoms than she had when she got the news. Each day she has been isolating herself from others and playing all her fears over and over in her mind. She has looked up all the negative things online about her sickness and is terrified by what she has been reading. She has tried to pray, begging God to please heal her, and going through phases of anger toward God that this is happening to her. Her conversations with friends and family members have been focused on all the things she needs to do to prepare for her death, how bad she feels every day, and which symptoms are now worse.

You may read this account and think, That's not me. However, does any of it look like your response? Maybe you believe everything in this book, and you pray in faith according to God's word, but then also give in to negative thoughts and doubt on days when your symptoms are worse. It is important for you to work on feeding on God's truth *and* avoiding any action that is a "fear/unbelief action."

Walking through the Valley of Sickness (in Faith):

Each day over the last four weeks, while the woman has experienced worsening symptoms, she has been immersing herself in the word of God. She reads God's word regarding healing and speaks those Scriptures over herself. She listens to praise music and reads testimonies of others being healed. When she wakes up in pain and thoughts of fear come or doubt comes because she isn't healed, she casts those thoughts down by speaking things like, "It doesn't matter what it looks like or how I feel, I am not moved by what I see. I believe God's word, and I am already healed. I wake up each day expecting to see my healing manifest. I WILL see the goodness of God and his promises come to pass in my life." Every time thoughts or symptoms come that are contrary to God's word, she refuses to accept them. She says out loud, "It is only a matter of time until I see the manifestation of my healing. God always honors his word, and healing is my covenant promise. I command all pain and every other symptom to leave my body in Jesus's name. Cancer cannot stay, God's word says so, and I am already healed." She spends time planning for her future, expecting that she will see her healing manifest. She speaks with her friends and family about the promises of God and tells them of all the stories she has read where God healed other people of cancer as well as other miraculous healings.

You can see the daily focus a person has and what they give their attention to when they walk in faith. Again, avoiding thinking, acting, and listening to things that bring doubt, unbelief, and death are *just as important* as feeding on things that bring faith. There is no room for unbelief! Your situation may be really bad, but if you are honest with yourself, having a complete meltdown does absolutely nothing for you. It doesn't make you feel better, and it doesn't change anything. In fact, the longer you allow yourself to behave in doubt and unbelief, the more you must overcome in your heart to get back in faith. If you have spent four weeks thinking (sowing into yourself) about how bad things are and that you are going to die, it will take effort to overcome all that negativity you fed into your spirit just to get to back to the place you were when you first heard the news! Refuse all that pity and fear, it is not from God, and you have too much on the line. Believe God and press in by standing on his word!

I Have Doubtful Thoughts, Does That Mean I Am Not in Faith?

NO! You are not out of faith if doubtful thoughts come. It is common to have doubtful thoughts; that is why Paul tells us to fight the good fight of faith in 1 Timothy 6:12. *Of course* you are going to have negative thoughts, and thoughts of unbelief will try to come in. Satan will work overtime to try to get you off the word of God. In the Parable of the Soils in Mark 4, verse 17 says that affliction or persecution comes for the word's sake. It comes for the word's sake because it is trying to stop the word from working, but the word works every time unless you back off the word.

68

It is absolutely normal to have to fight these thoughts, and every person will have to do it. Here are two things we must know about how to do this and be victorious:

1) We must cast the thought down. We basically deny its right to exist because God's word is the ultimate authority over all words or thoughts to its contrary. You don't counter a thought with another thought. You speak the truth of God's word out loud to break the power of that lie and to keep it from being a seed in your mind that would then get down into your heart.

"Casting down imaginations, and every high thing that exalteth itself against the knowledge of God, and bringing into captivity every thought to the obedience of Christ" (2 Corinthians 10:5).

2) We *take* a thought by *saying it*, whether it be a thought of unbelief or a thought of faith, the law works the same way. If you let yourself think about something repeatedly, that is when it will start coming out of your mouth. That is why you must cast the thoughts that are contrary to God's word down *immediately* and don't allow your mind to meditate on them, as noted in the first point. You don't let yourself keep pondering the

symptoms of your sickness or entertain the thought that you aren't healed when you haven't seen the results manifest yet. That is a lie: God's word says you are healed. If you keep thinking that way and don't cast it down, you will start speaking that as your truth! The last thing you want to do is *speak* unbelief, because the Bible says you *take* the thought by *saying* it. (That is why you counter the lies in your mind by *speaking* the word of God about your healing.) The following Scripture shows us that speaking a thought is how we *take* it.

"Therefore take no thought, saying, What shall we eat? or, What shall we drink? or, Wherewithal shall we be clothed?" (Matthew 6:31)

Faith "Works" (Actions) – Head Knowledge and Belief Are Not Enough.

We saw this component in the miracle progression, so let's talk more about what it is and its importance. You can read everything in this book, understand it, and believe it is all true and still not see results. How is that possible? Because faith without works is dead according to the Bible. It is *so important* not to miss this. Faith looks like action!

It is like building a house. You can have all the knowledge of how to build a house and understand how to do it. You can even have all the materials, but if you don't get up and *build the house*, it doesn't exist. Likewise, your healing will not manifest if you don't follow and act on the spiritual laws of healing. It's one thing to *have* faith; faith "works" are what you *do* with it.

Miracles Are Only Produced by Faith with Action.

Those actions are the things mentioned all throughout this book, such as following through with casting thoughts of unbelief down and speaking the word of God concerning you being healed (*doing it*); declaring that you are healed according to God's word and keep on declaring it, even if things appear worse for a season (*doing it*); actively forgiving people in your daily walk and being intentional about it (*doing it*); taking the time to study healing (*doing it*); and praising God that you are healed (*doing it*). There are many exercises outlined in the Healing Prescription chapter. Simply, you must act on (follow) the laws of healing to receive healing.

I want to say one more thing to encourage you here. It is normal to find yourself praying or quoting healing Scriptures (or other exercises in this book) and feel peace and faith come, and then not even ten minutes pass, and doubt and unbelief or feelings of discouragement come on you again. If that happens, and it probably will, it doesn't mean you are missing it! Just keep it up! You may find yourself pacing up and down your hallway speaking the word of God, sitting down, and then having to get right back up to do it again. Some days will be easier than others. The more you practice staying in faith and casting down the wrong thoughts, the easier it becomes. It *is* a fight you can win.

Can My Faith Heal Someone Else?

The answer is *yes*. I am including this chapter in the book because there are many people searching for answers because someone else in their life is sick. Not to mention that, as Christians, we are supposed to minister healing to others on a regular basis. Be sure to also go back and refresh yourself in the first chapter where we discussed the power and authority God gave us to heal. Here, we will discuss healing specifically as it relates to praying for and ministering healing to others in more depth. In the Bible, people *were* healed based on another person's faith, and we will be looking at these cases.

Remember, God shows no favoritism! If he does it for one person, he will do it for another if someone will reach out and believe it. *Someone's* faith must take it! Also, we need to get away from the dismissive thought, "Well, that was Jesus." Jesus came to show us what to do. We should expect to be more like him and press in to perfectly pattern what he did more and more each day of our walk. Are we Jesus? No, but he told us we will do his same works (and even greater!). We won't if we choose not to believe him. We must believe what Jesus said, and in order to believe that, we have to stop looking at our ability as "less than" as though there is no way we can be like him. We are *supposed* to be more and more like him!

"Verily, verily, I say unto you, He that believeth on me, the works that I do shall he do also; and greater works than these shall he do; because I go unto my Father" (John 14:12).

Case #1

Jesus healed the centurion's servant who was dying based on the centurion's faith. The account of this is in Matthew 8:5–13 and in Luke 7:1–10. Basically the centurion sent word to Jesus that he wanted him to heal his servant who was "sick of the palsy, grievously tormented" (Matthew 8:6), and "was sick, and ready to die" (Luke 7:2). *Now, watch this very closely...*

The account says that Jesus said he would come and heal the servant, but then the centurion said that Jesus just needed to speak the word only, and his servant would be healed. (Read the full account.) What Jesus said and did next is where we can settle in our hearts that it is *certain that another person can be healed based on our faith.*

"When Jesus heard it, he marvelled, and said to them that followed, Verily I say unto you, I have not found so great faith, no, not in Israel" (Matthew 8:10).

❖ Jesus actually marveled at the centurion's faith (not the sick person's faith). Needless to say, this man actually impressed Jesus greatly by his faith. *Now watch this. . .*

"And Jesus said unto the centurion, Go thy way; and as thou hast believed, so be it done unto thee. And his servant was healed in the selfsame hour" (Matthew 8:13).

❖ "As *thou* hast believed"—this is clearly stating that the miracle was granted based on the centurion's faith alone.

❖ "So be it done unto *thee*"—the miracle was done unto the centurion (again, based on his faith). The miracle manifested healing in someone else, but it was done (granted) unto the centurion.

❖ This was not an account of a specific miracle that God instructed Jesus to do. This miracle was granted because the *centurion* desired the miracle, and the centurion had faith on behalf of the person who needed the miracle. This did not happen because God wanted the servant well (although he wants everyone well); again, it happened because the centurion put a demand on the healing with his faith out of his desire to see the person made well. And we can do the same for those we desire to see well.

Case #2

This is the account of the paralyzed man that was healed when brought in on a mat and lowered through the roof by others to get to Jesus. It is found in Matthew 9:1–8, Mark 2:1–12, and Luke 5:17–25.

Basically, it says the men could not get the sick (paralyzed) man to Jesus because of the crowd, so they did whatever was necessary to reach Jesus in their faith. They got up on the roof and lowered the man down to Jesus! *Now watch this...*

"And Jesus seeing their faith" (Matthew 9:2).

❖ This points directly to *their* faith, the men that brought the paralyzed man to him.

❖ Jesus went on to tell the paralyzed man (right after he saw the other men's faith) that his sins were forgiven him, and then later in the passage told him to arise and take up his bed, which he did. However, the point in this is that it only references the fact that Jesus saw the other men's faith, and thus that was all that was required. If the paralyzed man had to have the faith the other men did, or if the paralyzed man did have the same faith as the other men, and it was the paralyzed man's faith that caused him to receive the healing, Jesus would have said that directly (as he did in other passages where people received their healing based on their own faith). Jesus is our teacher. We must have faith that Jesus is a good teacher and will tell us things specifically if they are required. Why would he not? He commanded us to heal the sick, as we have seen earlier in this book; therefore, he would and has given us all knowledge in his word to carry out the commandments he has given us. (As well as the power to do it.)

Case #3

The leper that received healing is found in Matthew 8:2–4, Mark 1:40–44, and Luke 5:12–14. This is quite a simple account of this man's healing:

"And, behold, there came a leper and worshipped him, saying, Lord, if thou wilt, thou canst make me clean. And Jesus put forth his hand, and touched him, saying, I will; be thou clean. And immediately his leprosy was cleansed" (Matthew 8:2–3).

- ❖ This man did not have the "faith that takes it" and was healed on Jesus's faith, not his own. He approached Jesus believing he *could* heal him, but he was not in faith that he *would* heal him.

- ❖ Jesus did not tell this man that he must take his healing by faith by instructing or correcting him that he needed to first believe he would be healed in order to be healed because the only way to receive healing would be on his own faith.

- ❖ Jesus just healed him when he openly approached Jesus for healing even though the man did not have the faith on his own to receive it. Therefore, we as Christians can also minister healing for others with our faith when they are open to God's healing and desire it.

Case #4

The epileptic boy that was healed is found in Matthew 17:14–21, Mark 9:14–29, and Luke 9:37–42. So, this account is of a father bringing his son to Jesus after he brought him to the disciples and they could not cure him. There is *a lot* we need to look at in this account, so I am including it in its entirety. Read the passage carefully, and then we will break the important points down.

And when he came to his disciples, he saw a great multitude about them, and the scribes questioning with them. And straightway all the people, when they beheld him, were greatly amazed, and running to him saluted him. And he asked the scribes, What question ye with them? And one of the multitude answered and said, Master, I have brought unto thee my son, which hath a dumb spirit; And wheresoever he taketh him, he teareth him: and he foameth, and gnasheth with his teeth, and pineth away: and I spake to thy disciples that they should cast him out; and they could not. He answereth him, and saith, O faithless generation, how long shall I be with you? how long shall I suffer you? bring him unto me. And they brought him unto him: and when he saw him, straightway the spirit tare him; and he fell on the ground, and wallowed foaming. And he asked his father, How long is it ago since this came unto him? And he said, Of a child. And ofttimes it hath cast him into the fire, and into the waters, to destroy him: but if thou canst do any thing, have compassion on us, and help us. Jesus said unto him, If thou canst believe, all things are possible to him that believeth. And straightway the father of the child cried out, and said with tears, Lord, I believe; help thou mine unbelief. When Jesus saw that the people came running together, he rebuked the foul spirit, saying unto him, Thou dumb and deaf spirit, I charge thee, come out of him, and enter no more into him. And the spirit cried, and rent him sore, and came out of him: and he was as one dead; insomuch that many said, He is dead. But Jesus took him by the hand, and lifted him up; and he arose. And when he was come into the house, his disciples asked him privately, Why could not we cast him out? And he said unto them, This kind can come forth by nothing, but by prayer and fasting. (Mark 9:14–29)

What is this telling us?

❖ First of all, the boy himself did not get healed on his own faith. Nowhere does it ever show that the boy had any faith for his own healing, but the father is the one who was reaching out to Jesus on his behalf.

❖ The father did not have the faith for the boy to be healed either! He said to Jesus, "But if thou canst do any thing, have compassion on us, and help us." This is *not* faith that takes it. Now, Jesus did respond, "If thou canst believe, all things *are* possible to him that believeth." However, here he was telling the man that anyone who had this faith could do what Jesus was doing, and the boy was healed on Jesus's faith because the man answered back, "Lord, I believe; help thou mine unbelief." This shows us that faith and unbelief can exist at the same time, but that is for another topic. Sticking to the fact that others can be healed based on our faith, we see that the man never came to a place of "faith that takes it," and more importantly the boy who was the one who was sick did not act on any faith. Nowhere does Jesus say the boy was healed on his faith. This is another account where Jesus healed someone based on Jesus's faith, not the faith of the sick person (which we have been given the command and power to do as well), when the person sought out the healing and was open to it.

❖ Here is something interesting directed at those administering the healing: Jesus was *not happy* that the disciples were unable to deliver the boy. He expected them to be able to heal this boy, period. Read the following again, and we will then look at this fact in more depth because it is important to us who are believing for others to be healed. Let's look at it in Matthew's account:

"And I brought him to thy disciples, and they could not cure him. Then Jesus answered and said, O faithless and perverse generation, how long shall I be with you?

how long shall I suffer you? bring him hither to me"
(Matthew 17:16–17).

❖ When the father told Jesus that the disciples
   could not cure his son, Jesus wasn't just annoyed,
   he was really upset at that. He called his disciples
   "faithless" and a "perverse generation"! He
   basically went on to say, "How long do I have to
   deal with you or put up with you?" As in, "Why
   haven't you gotten this?!"

❖ This clearly tells us as Christians that God
   expects us to be able to do these things. There is
   no question of should we, are we able, or
   anything of the like. The response of Jesus to his
   followers being unable to manifest the miracle
   was major frustration. How could we ever think
   that we are not to minister healing and
   deliverance and see it work? Jesus was not
   having it when it didn't work!!

Okay, but it is also important for us to understand as
Christians ministering healing or any other
miracle *why* it didn't work. Let's look at that now:

Then came the disciples to Jesus apart, and said,
Why could not we cast him out? And Jesus said unto
them, Because of your unbelief: for verily I say unto
you, If ye have faith as

a grain of mustard seed, ye shall say unto this mountain, Remove hence to yonder place; and it shall remove; and nothing shall be impossible unto you. Howbeit this kind goeth not out but by prayer and fasting. (Matthew 17:19–21)

❖ First things first, Jesus said the disciples could not manifest the miracle (as they had been commanded) because of *their* unbelief. He did not say they were unsuccessful because of the boy's unbelief (and the passage doesn't say the boy had any faith). He did not say it was because of the boy's father's unbelief (and the passage shows clearly he did not have the faith that takes possession of healing). If the manifestation would only happen if the person who needed healing had faith, then Jesus would have said this when the disciples *directly* asked *why* it didn't work!! He also did not say only he himself (Jesus) could do it. He said it was because of *their* unbelief.

❖ The disciples were surprised that they could not minister the miracle! Remember, they had already been performing miracles, and that is why they asked Jesus why they couldn't do it in this case.

❖ Something important we see as Christians ministering healing is that Jesus said "this kind" didn't go but by prayer and fasting. He was *not* talking about a demon here; he was talking about unbelief. This tells us that there is certain unbelief we can't overcome and get rid of in our walk of faith without incorporating fasting into our lives! This is a teaching moment to us who are believing for healing for others!! This is a fact: if we aren't fasting regularly, we should be! If the disciples weren't an exception to this, neither are we.

There are more cases of people receiving healing throughout the Bible where they did not clearly have the faith to take the healing on their own. Another thing to contemplate is that there is more than one account where multitudes of people needed healing, and Jesus healed them all!! There is no way every single one of those people came to "faith that takes it" on their own to receive their healing. I believe they must have been open to receive, as we have seen in some of these instances and in other cases in the word, but it is extremely unlikely they were all healed on their own faith in these multitude accounts. If they weren't healed on their own faith, and faith is necessary for miracles to manifest, they had to have been healed on Jesus's faith (which means people can also be healed on our faith).

What If the Person I Am Praying for Has Unbelief?

This is a common question, and one that we, as Christians, really need to know the answer to based on what the word says so our faith won't be hindered when we pray for others. A person *can* be healed on *your* faith.

❖ We don't discount the Scriptures (and there are many) that say, "Your faith has made you whole," or "According to your faith, be it unto you." This can exist and is truth, while not always being necessary if there is *more than one way a person receives healing.* Christians can and do receive healing (and any other promise) when they take possession of the promise in their own faith. I have heard pastors call this kind of faith "faith that takes it." Jesus never said things for "filler," he made a point to say these things to people so they (and we) would know that that is how the miracle happened. Why did he want us to know that? Because we are supposed to see these miracles in our everyday lives, and we need to understand how that happens to see them manifest. It is God's highest desire that individuals understand his word and know how to receive what they need on their own faith, but that is not the *only* way it happens.

Again, the Scriptures evidencing people who received their miracle based on *their* faith show us *that* method of receiving healing. It does not mean it is the only method, and Jesus never said anywhere that it was the only method. If we trust God that he has written us an instruction manual, wouldn't he clearly state that this is the only way a person would receive healing if that were the case? In addition to this, we see other healing miracles that manifested based on either the faith of Jesus or someone else (or both) on behalf of the sick person and have included the different methods of healing earlier in this book.

What about When Jesus Couldn't Heal People in His Hometown Because of Their Unbelief?

Yes, we must address this because the word does say this! Let's look at exactly what it says so we can understand how their unbelief hindered Jesus from being able to perform miracles on behalf of the people.

And he went out from thence, and came into his own country; and his disciples follow him. And when the sabbath day was come, he began to teach in the synagogue: and many hearing him were astonished, saying, From whence hath this man these things? and what wisdom is this which is given unto him, that even such mighty works are wrought by his hands? Is not this the carpenter, the son of Mary, the brother of James, and Joses, and of Juda, and Simon? and are not his sisters here with us? And they were offended at him. But Jesus said unto them, A prophet is not without honour, but in his own country, and among his own kin, and in his own house. And he could there do no mighty work, save that he laid his hands upon a few sick folk, and healed them. And he marvelled because of their unbelief. (Mark 6:1–6)

❖ Yes, it says Jesus *could not* (not that he *would not*) do any mighty works. Therefore, the word clearly tells us that the people blocked his power to heal, and in these types of circumstances, unbelief would affect us ministering healing the exact same way.

❖ We reconcile this account with the others already noted in this way: there are different *kinds* of unbelief!! Jesus already told us that in the account noted regarding the epileptic boy. What we see in this passage is that the people had a different attitude than other people who did get healed even when they didn't have "faith that takes it." These people (by their comments) were basically stating, "Who does he think he is? Isn't this just the carpenter, Mary's son?" Then it goes further to say that they were "offended at him." They didn't just struggle to believe that it was possible to be healed supernaturally or wonder if it was God's will to actually heal them, they outright *mocked* Jesus, *rejected* him, and became *offended at him!* For a person who reacts this way, we will not be able to minister healing to them, and this type of unbelief will not allow us to operate in the power of God on their behalf. If it wouldn't work for Jesus, it won't work for us. At the same time, we have seen many accounts in the word where people were healed on someone else's faith, which means they did not have the faith to receive it for themselves. If the person is open and receiving the gospel you preach, and desires God to heal them, even if they struggle to get to the place of "faith that takes it" on their own, they can be healed based on your faith.

Remember the centurion, and go before God based on that word! If he did it for the centurion, his law would have to also give you the same result. What did Jesus say to the centurion regarding healing his servant? "Go thy way; and as thou hast believed, so be it done unto thee" (Matthew 8:13).

Things That Block Healing

There is more than one way a miracle can be aborted. Different things happen with people that can stop the manifestation from occurring in their lives.

#1 Unbelief

Unbelief is a miracle killer. This is clearly already evident based on the examples and Scriptures noted so far throughout this book. Remember, the *only* time Jesus did *not* perform miracles, it was due to the people's unbelief. In every other account, he healed people (or delivered them, etc.). "And he did not many mighty works there because of their unbelief" (Matthew 8:13).

With that being said, if you still wonder if it's God's will to heal you, or if you think sometimes he heals and sometimes he doesn't, remember there was not a single instance where it was not the will of God to heal anyone. Not one. Nor were there any instances where he said they were sick to teach them something. Nor was there an account of anyone needing to be sick a while longer before they could be healed to teach them anything or as a punishment. Nor do you see anywhere that God didn't heal because the person didn't deserve it or deserved to be sick. Again, the *only time* Jesus did not heal was when the *people* wouldn't receive because of their unbelief.

This also supports what we have noted previously in The Laws of Healing. That it was up to the people to believe and be healed, it was not up to God whether they were healed or not.

Let's look at the account of Peter walking on water and how unbelief *stopped* the miracle he was *already* experiencing right in its tracks.

And when he [Jesus] sent the multitudes away, he went up into a mountain apart to pray: and when the evening was come, he was there alone. But the ship was now in the midst of the sea, tossed with waves: for the wind was contrary. And in the fourth watch of the night Jesus went unto them, walking on the sea. And when the disciples saw him walking on the sea, they were troubled, saying, It is a spirit; and they cried out for fear. But straightway Jesus spake unto them, saying, Be of good cheer; it is I; be not afraid. And Peter answered him and said, Lord, if it be thou, bid me come unto thee on the water. And he said, Come. And when Peter was come down out of the ship, he walked on the water, to go to Jesus. But when he saw the wind boisterous, he was afraid; and beginning to sink, he cried, saying, Lord, save me. And immediately Jesus stretched forth his hand, and caught him, and said unto him, O thou of little faith, wherefore didst thou doubt? And when they were come into the ship, the wind ceased. Then they that were in the ship came and worshipped him, saying, Of a truth thou art the Son of God. (Matthew 14:23–33)

Peter was able to walk on the water *until he put his eyes on the outside circumstances.* Notice it says, "When he saw the boisterous wind." That was what made him afraid, and when he became afraid, he began to sink. Jesus then said, "O thou of little faith, wherefore didst thou doubt?" What do we get from this?

- ❖ Peter was outright defying natural laws and experiencing a supernatural miracle.
- ❖ Peter then put his eyes on outward circumstances that "said" to him that what he was doing was impossible.
- ❖ Looking and focusing on these contrary circumstances caused doubt and unbelief to be sown into his heart.
- ❖ The presence of doubt and unbelief in his heart stopped the miracle.

It is imperative to apply this to your own situation. We clearly see from this account that unbelief stops miracles, no question. However, *we also see* that looking at the circumstances is how the unbelief can get in. When you are dealing with a sickness, many times you will have physical symptoms of that sickness (maybe even extreme symptoms), and you may also be getting negative reports from your doctor. You must get your mind off all of that, completely ignore it, and focus on the fact that God's word is sure, and it says you are healed.

Look at the ways you have been allowing doubt and unbelief in. How often have you been thinking about those negative things throughout the day? You have to think about what you've been thinking about! How often have you been having doom and gloom conversations with others regarding what you are dealing with? You must stop all that, immediately. Don't give doubt and unbelief any place in you! You have a choice to make, it is up to you to make it.

#2 Unforgiveness

Unforgiveness in your heart is serious, and it blocks your prayers and kills miracles. Period. You must deal with it; you cannot let it continue. It is a sin not to forgive someone, no matter what they have done to you or someone you care about. This may be easier for some of us to say and do than it is for others. People who have had serious wrongs done to them may really struggle with this. Unforgiveness is a prison, and it will poison your heart. Forgiving is for *you*; it is not for the other person. Sometimes we have to forgive by faith.

What does that mean? It means you decide with your will to forgive someone, you pray, and say you forgive and release them, even when you don't feel like you have forgiven them. That is where the faith comes in. Eventually, by continuing to release them every time they come to your mind or you think negatively about them, your feelings will catch up, and you will be free from that bondage in your own heart. When you begin to do this, you must make a conscious effort to change your thoughts toward that person and to stop speaking anything negatively about them at all.

Still don't think forgiveness is that big of a deal? Well . . .

And Jesus answering saith unto them, Have faith in God. For verily I say unto you, That whosoever shall say unto this mountain, Be thou removed, and be thou cast into the sea; and shall not doubt in his heart, but shall believe that those things which he saith shall come to pass; he shall have whatsoever he saith. Therefore I say unto you, What things soever ye desire, when ye pray, believe that ye receive them, and ye shall have them. *And when ye stand praying, forgive, if ye have ought against any:* that your Father also which is in heaven may forgive you your trespasses. (Mark 11:22–25, emphasis added)

Notice the last part where Jesus mentioned forgiveness *right after* he told us how to pray and believe to receive miracles. There is a reason he said this about forgiveness when telling us how to pray for the things we have need of, and that is because it is relevant to being able to receive those things we are praying for.

#3 Violating Natural Healing Laws

This one is not fun, but it is the truth. The Bible says a man reaps what he sows. If you are having all kinds of medical issues due to your weight, yes, God loves you, and he will heal you, but those medical problems will keep coming back if you don't take steps to follow the natural laws of healing and lose weight. Why? Because they are stemming from something being out of order in the natural realm. We cannot use a healing miracle to override the natural laws God set forth to take care of our bodies and expect it to work continually while we refuse to change.

It is important not to get into condemnation in this area. Sometimes we aren't taking care of our bodies because we are being lazy. In those cases, when a health problem presents itself, we just need to correct the problem. Other times we neglect the natural laws because we have addictions. We may smoke because we are addicted, some may drink excessive alcohol in an addiction, others may be either eating extremely unhealthy food due to addiction or are overweight because of what they are eating (or both), etc.

God wants us to realize that we don't have to be perfect to receive healing from him! We will go more in depth on this next, but the key factor is that our hearts must be right toward God. There are some things we can't change without his help. I believe the first step in correcting this area that is out of order is repenting before God and acknowledging we have been violating his instruction. If it is an area you have total control over, then it is time to make the proper changes and position yourself to receive your miracle (along with the other things in this book). If it is an area that you struggle in, like with an addiction, then your responsibility is the same: acknowledge that and repent before God.

You can't stop there, however. Next you need to do the things you *can do* in this area and begin to study and press into your relationship with God for deliverance and his help. If making the corrections in this area of the natural laws of healing would heal the ailment, my advice would be to spend equal amounts of time digging into deliverance from the addictions and digging into the emotional healing needed, which you are doing right now in your quest for a healing miracle. You can't sit back and do nothing. Remember, God looks at the heart. There are things you can do, and if you are unwilling to do those things, then you are purposely opening the door to sickness by violating the laws that govern natural health and by refusing to take responsibility for what you can change or the steps you can take.

#4 Sin and Disobedience

This is another tough one, but we need to have the proper view on this. If we are not careful, we will get under the law instead of under grace where we belong. At the same time, it is important to understand what it means to be under grace.

Being under grace does not mean we can keep on sinning and expect God's miracles to flow freely in our lives. They do still manifest many times because of God's grace and mercy. However, that is different than standing in faith and following God's laws of healing, which causes the healing miracle to manifest as a covenant promise, as shown in the progression and components of a miracle we have looked at.

Again, the Bible says we reap what we sow. Sin brings death and destruction and opens the door to the devil in our lives here on earth, even after we are saved! There is a difference between living an imperfect life (which is all of us) in a constant state of communion, continual repentance, and change in our relationship with God, and continual sin that we refuse to deal with or repent of. We never lose our salvation, but there are consequences to our sin, and many sins open the door for physical sickness and disease in our bodies.

"Be not deceived; God is not mocked: for whatsoever a man soweth, that shall he also reap. For he that soweth to his flesh shall of the flesh reap corruption; but he that soweth to the Spirit shall of the Spirit reap life everlasting" (Galatians 6:7–8).

Again, this is all about our heart toward God. Do not get into condemnation over this! There are many things people struggle with that they need deliverance from and God's help to overcome. You can receive your healing miracle right in the middle of your sin, it is where you are in your heart and your commitment in your relationship with God in dealing with it that matter.

If you have had continual sin in your life or have disobeyed what God has told you to do, it is time to repent. Stop the sin. If you can't stop the sin on your own, make a commitment to God to start walking out your deliverance with him because that is something you *can* do. If God has told you to do something, and you are just in outright disobedience by willful choice, repent and do what he told you to do.

With all of this noted, people are held accountable on different levels in relation to where they are in their walk with God and their understanding. The man at the pool of Bethesda did not have to "get it right" before receiving his miracle, but Jesus warned him after his healing that if he didn't, a worse thing would come upon him. The entire account is in John 5:2–14, but let's just look at the final verse for this point. Notice, dealing with the sin was *so important* that Jesus *went back to find him* later, after he was healed, to tell him to deal with his sin so he could remain whole. "Afterward Jesus findeth him in the temple, and said unto him, Behold, thou art made whole: sin no more, lest a worse thing come unto thee" (John 5:14).

This tells us there is definitely a link to sin and disease, and we are expected to deal with the sin to close the open door, or else we give it legal authority to stay. You can't cast something out when it has legal authority to be there. You must take its authority away first, and then it can be removed. Remember, once you have repented, that is it! It's over, there isn't a long time you have to wait or a consequence that must be paid for your healing: it was already paid for by Jesus. When you repent and deal with the sin, that is it right that second because you have appropriated the blood of Jesus.

Let's be clear, you don't earn your healing. Jesus is the one that did that. It is impossible for you to earn your healing. One sin ever committed disqualifies you and opens the door to the wages of sin, which is death in your life. No amount of good deeds will wipe that sin away, period. There is no earning anything, we can only accept that Jesus earned it and paid for it on our behalf.

At the same time, we have a level of responsibility in receiving this free gift, and it is important to see the difference. Let me reiterate because this is such a fine line: we are not under the law but under grace, and this place of grace appropriation is tied to our heart toward God in our walk with him. Again, you can still struggle with a sin in your life and receive your healing. You just can't ignore the sin, refuse to bring it before the Lord, and receive his help to deal with it.

#5 A Person's Will

If a person does not desire to be healed, prayer for that healing is fruitless. The same way God will not override a person's will regarding salvation, his laws will not violate their will regarding receiving their healing. This is important to understand especially when we are praying for other people.

#6 Not Walking in Love, and Faith Actions

While these are listed on the "receiving" portion of the miracle progression, it does not hurt to look at them more closely, because if we fail to implement them, our faith won't work, and we won't see healing manifest.

If you aren't walking in love, everything else is pointless. This is more than getting past unforgiveness. It is an everyday intentional walk of focusing on loving others. Below, I emphasized the verse in relation to faith to move mountains (miracle-working faith), but the entire passage is important (the word "charity" means love):

> Though I speak with the tongues of men and of angels, and have not charity, I am become as sounding brass, or a tinkling cymbal. And though I have the gift of prophecy, and understand all mysteries, and all knowledge; *and though I have all faith, so that I could remove mountains, and have not charity, I am nothing.* And though I bestow all my goods to feed the poor, and though I give my body to be burned, and have not charity, it profiteth me nothing. Charity suffereth long, and is kind; charity envieth not; charity vaunteth not itself, is not puffed up, Doth not behave itself unseemly, seeketh not her own, is not easily provoked, thinketh no evil; Rejoiceth not in iniquity, but rejoiceth in the truth; Beareth all things, believeth all things, hopeth all things, endureth all things. Charity never faileth. (1 Corinthians 13:1–8)

Next, regarding our faith works (actions), we clearly see their importance in James.

What doth it profit, my brethren, though a man say he hath faith, and have not works? can faith save him? If a brother or sister be naked, and destitute of daily food, And one of you say unto them, Depart in peace, be ye warmed and filled; notwithstanding ye give them not those things which are needful to the body; what doth it profit? Even so faith, if it hath not works, is dead, being alone. Yea, a man may say, Thou hast faith, and I have works: shew me thy faith without thy works, and I will shew thee my faith by my works. Thou believest that there is one God; thou doest well: the devils also believe, and tremble. But wilt thou know, O vain man, that faith without works is dead? Was not Abraham our father justified by works, when he had offered Isaac his son upon the altar? Seest thou how faith wrought with his works, and by works was faith made perfect? (James 2:14–22)

It can't be any more in our face than that. Faith without corresponding action does absolutely nothing. He told us that it profits nothing and that it is as dead as your body will be when your spirit has departed. You may be asking, What exactly are faith actions? We go over this elsewhere in the book, but in summary, examples would look like this:

- ❖ When you don't see the manifestation of healing yet and may be experiencing symptoms, you call those things that are not as though they are (that is what the Bible says). You make faith declarations, such as, "I know it may look like I am still sick, but I refuse to believe that. God's word says I am healed, and I am already healed."
- ❖ You plan your future as though you are already healed.
- ❖ Your conversations with others are focused on how good God is and how he has already healed you.
- ❖ If you can't move your legs, you keep trying to move them several times a day, declaring, "Legs, I command you to move, you will move and function properly and be whole right now because God has already healed me."
- ❖ You meditate on what your life looks like as if it were whole of the sickness.

After reading these Scriptures, it is apparent that these two things, walking in love and the corresponding faith actions, are the "fuel source" for faith. Likewise, it is also apparent that faith goes absolutely nowhere without working in tandem with these two things.

Additional Teaching From Jesus

We see some of the miracle killers in the Parable of the Soils in Matthew 13. Jesus explained this to us and in verse 18 he said, "Hear ye therefore the parable of the sower," and then he continued . . .

Soil #1

"When any one heareth the word of the kingdom, and understandeth it not, then cometh the wicked one, and catcheth away that which was sown in his heart. This is he which received seed by the way side" (Matthew 13:19).

The reason this type of person can't receive a miracle manifestation is because he does not understand the word (the seed) on healing. If he doesn't understand the word, he will never learn to make it work in his life. He hears it, and it goes right over his head. Jesus even notes here that the "wicked one" (Satan) comes and steals it away from that person's heart, and it is gone immediately. It never makes any sense at all to him in a way that he fully sees the spiritual truth. This ties into the first component listed in the miracle progression, which we have gone over.

In this instance, the only real way to get past this place is to take the time to know the word. Listen to teachings, read the Bible, and talk with other believers about what it is you are facing and what the word says about it. You have to make the time, and you have to make it a priority. God is faithful. If you don't understand, ask God to reveal it to you, and he will, but you must make the effort to engage.

Soil #2

"But he that received the seed into stony places, the same is he that heareth the word, and anon with joy receiveth it; Yet hath he not root in himself, but dureth for a while: for when tribulation or persecution ariseth because of the word, by and by he is offended" (Matthew 13:20–21).

The reason this type of person can't receive a miracle manifestation is because he has no "root." Think of a new plant just planted. If you pull hard enough on that plant before the roots have started to take hold in the soil, it will give and come right out of the ground. God is using this to show us that when the truth (the healing promise in the word) comes into this person, they hear it and even become excited because they believe it. Okay, so this person has the vehicle (faith) required to receive the miracle! However, when trouble arises or they don't see the answer (miracle) immediately, they lose faith, and the word itself that was planted is ripped from their heart. When the word is ripped up, then they have moved out of their position to receive the miracle. These are the people who have faith initially, but they don't *stand* in faith (or stay in faith).

This is a pretty common occurrence, and you have to train yourself through this place. You must *practice* staying in faith, and the more you practice, the easier it becomes. Notice it says tribulation or persecution arises *because of the word*. Jesus was telling us that when we start getting serious about the fight in the spiritual realm, we will face opposition. And he also told us that the opposition comes because of the word! It is there to stop the word from manifesting the promises of God in your life and the lives of those you love! Satan wouldn't come after the word if it had no power or threat to his kingdom. You must learn to stick with and continue to profess God's word no matter what the situation looks like.

Soil #3

"He also that received seed among the thorns is he that heareth the word; and the care of this world, and the deceitfulness of riches, choke the word, and he becometh unfruitful" (Matthew 13:22).

This person is the type that may have faith to hear, receive, and believe the word that the miracle will come to pass. They may also have the faith to stand and see it through. This person is not losing the miracle because of the opposition or because not seeing the manifestation right away causes them not to *believe* and get into doubt. This person loses the miracle manifestation because they get distracted and concerned with the cares of this world, riches, or whatever else Satan can grab their attention with. In this instance, it is not the absence of faith, nor the presence of unbelief or doubt, that renders the word ineffectual and kills the miracle. It is distraction: other things pulling this person's focus off standing on the word and pursuing that miracle in the spirit to see it manifest.

Reading what Jesus said about all of this, we see that Satan tries to steal the word immediately so people never understand how to operate in spiritual things and be successful. If that doesn't work, and they believe the word, then he brings opposition and tribulation, trying to get them to lose their faith in the word itself (God) so they won't be effective. If that still doesn't work, and he can't get them to not believe God, then he attempts to get them focused on something else, going in another direction, or not paying attention.

The bottom line is this: if you hear the word, and you take the time to understand it, Satan can't steal it from your heart. And then you press in and practice staying in faith and implementing God's laws of healing no matter what the situation looks like. And then if you stay in that place of pressing in and not allowing yourself to be busy or distracted from seeing the miracle come to pass, you are going to see it manifest. Satan knows that, and that is why he tries these different angles to "muddy up the water," so to speak, so that you can't figure out why you aren't seeing what God said you would see. Now let's look at what Jesus said next . . .

Soil #4

"But he that received seed into the good ground is he that heareth the word, and understandeth it; which also beareth fruit, and bringeth forth, some an hundredfold, some sixty, some thirty" (Matthew 13:23).

In the previous verses Jesus referred to the heart of people receiving the seed. The seed is the word of God that promises a certain outcome for your situation. In those three cases he mentioned one person receiving the seed (word) by the wayside, one receiving the word in a stony heart, and one receiving the word in a heart with thorns. "Good ground" in this verse is referencing the "soil" of the heart of this person and is letting us know that the issues present in those other cases are not present in the heart of this person that actually receives the miracle or "bears fruit." Thus, this person hears the word, understands it, and does not lose faith or get distracted away from receiving their miracle like the other people did.

Seeing the Miracle

All these things play a role in whether or not we will see the miracle we are believing for manifest in our lives in the natural realm. Until we make these things habit and begin to practice them on a regular basis, our success in this area will be nonexistent, or at best, extremely limited.

If you have never experienced pushing through in the spirit to actually see the thing you were praying for manifest, how much time are you in the word? Are you staying in faith and not speaking doubt? Are your daily actions those of faith, believing you were already healed and expecting to see it manifest? If you only pray here and there or you only read the word sporadically concerning the issue, that is most likely the biggest place you are missing it.

You have to be intentional by getting focused on the word of God concerning the matter. As Creflo Dollar said, you have to keep your faith on the field! God will honor his word and will not fail to perform it. Don't accept anything less than what he has promised!

Healing Assessments

In this chapter, we are going to get a baseline of where you are and discover which areas need work to better position yourself to see your healing manifest. While outlining the current prognosis or symptoms you are experiencing is good so you can document your healing, the most important thing when standing for a miracle is reviewing what beliefs you are holding in your heart and how you are applying the spiritual laws related to healing.

You can make a copy of the assessments or get a sheet of paper and answer the questions by number and date the assessment. It would be good to go back and retake these assessments regularly to see what progress you are making in walking out your healing miracle.

Assessment 1 – Prognosis, Symptoms, and Progress

For this first assessment, document where you are right now. There is no questionnaire included here. Just note the ailment(s) you've been dealing with, along with all symptoms and their frequency in whatever method you choose. Don't spend a lot of time, just make quick, clear notes, as we are not focusing on the problem. You will want to update this as you go forward with progress because that is what it's for! At the bottom of the assessment, write a paragraph defining the healing you are believing God for. Be sure to date the original assessment and all progress updates.

Here's an example list of what you would include in each prognosis, symptom, and progress assessment:

- ❖ Title Assessment (Prognosis, Symptoms, and Progress)
- ❖ Name and Date
- ❖ Prognosis/Doctor's Diagnosis (You don't have to list this on updates unless you have received a new diagnosis since the last assessment.)
- ❖ Symptoms of Ailment(s) (List all symptoms you have had since the last assessment.)
- ❖ Other Details (Such as when the diagnosis was given and when listed symptoms started.)
- ❖ Paragraph (State what you are believing God for! Be specific about the healing you want. In assessment updates, note improvements that you have seen since the last assessment.)

Assessment 2 – My Beliefs

This assessment is designed to show where your heart is in relation to your actual beliefs. Answer honestly and mark "No," "Maybe," or "Yes" according to what you believe right now regarding each statement.

DATE: _____

Belief Statement Assessment	No	Maybe	Yes
1) I believe it is God's will to heal me, and it is always his will to heal.			
2) I believe I am healed, and I *will* see the healing manifest.			
3) I believe God wants to see my healing manifest more than I do, and I don't have to beg or convince him.			
4) I believe Jesus already purchased my healing by the stripes he took on his back at the cross.			
5) I believe my healing is manifesting no matter what symptoms I experience or reports I receive to the contrary.			
6) I believe that God has already healed me, and I don't have to earn it.			
7) I believe I have access to all of God's healing power within me, and I can release it when I choose.			

This assessment does not have scoring. You either believe the statement, you don't, or are in the middle, building faith for it. It is *imperative* that you believe the truths of God's word, otherwise it will affect your faith to receive your healing. If you find that you cannot honestly say yes to each of these statements, then you need to address that belief in your heart until you can.

For the first statement, "I believe it is God's will to heal me, and it's always his will to heal," it may be simple for you to answer yes without hesitation after you have read so much about the word that clearly shows it is his will.

The more difficult belief statements to answer yes to will most likely be the ones stating that the healing has already taken place and will manifest, no question. For so many of us, we can get to the place where we know it is God's will to heal, and we can even get our heart to the place where we believe he heals every time because we see it in the word. And yet, we struggle with stating with certainty that *our* healing will manifest.

If this is you, don't be discouraged! Every single Christian must combat unbelief for any miracle they are believing God for, whether it's healing or something else. That is just part of it. The reason these assessments are here is to help you get straight to the heart of the matter! The faster you get clarity on any issues in your heart, the faster you can fix them.

How do you fix them? With the methods lined out in this book showing you how to feed your faith and starve your doubts. As you actually implement the different laws and exercises, they will change the belief in your heart (God's word supernaturally does this). Faith will begin to come, doubt will begin to go, and your answers to the belief statements will reflect that. You can also begin the practice of simply stating the belief and then say, "That's true, and I choose to believe that."

Assessment 3 – My Spiritual Growth

These next questions will help you form a clearer picture of how well you are actually *implementing* God's healing laws in your everyday life. There is a *direct connection* between miracle manifestation and the items noted in the assessment. The fact is that if you are believing God's word for healing (especially for a major sickness), you aren't going to be able to walk in faith if you are only feeding your spirit what is needed a couple times a month. That is just not feasible, and that is not what God's laws regarding healing tell us.

Healing, or any other promise in God's word, is not received by getting into legalism. There is no set formula or rule to how many times you do what, so we need to be careful not to get into that mindset. We are not "working" to be healed. As in, we don't get healed because we read our Bible and pray several times a day. We get healed because it is already available because of what Jesus did. The time we are spending is not "earning" the miracle or making it happen. The time we are spending is preparing our heart with understanding and building faith, because when that is present, and we act on it, the miracles flow like God said they would. If we were already at that place of faith in our heart, we would just speak a word like Jesus did and see the miracle manifest immediately. We aren't working to get "gold stars" with our deeds to get healed.

We do, however, have the guidelines God gave us in his word to see miracles manifest, and he spelled those laws out to us for a reason. He doesn't do anything without a purpose. Remember, God *provided* healing for anyone who would receive it, but *we* still have to do the receiving! That is what the whole purpose of this book is. Not just to learn about healing, but to be healed!

Other Notes before Taking This Assessment:

❖ You will notice that some items listed that lower the overall score are items you can't control (such as how often you experience physical symptoms). You can't help that, but they are listed there to help you see what is fed into your spirit regularly so you know how it effects your faith and unbelief.

❖ Do not get into condemnation about any item you feel you can't answer with a score you feel you *should* have. The goal is to grow in faith, and the questions are tools to get you to think about what you are doing daily to help that.

❖ I am highlighting here again that we are not to get into works with this! It is a tool to help us see what is not seen with the natural eyes.

❖ Be sure to make a copy of this assessment and use the copy to mark your answers. You will want to retake this assessment periodically throughout your healing journey. Remember, the purpose of this book is to be a tool to *implement* the healing laws, according to the word of God, in your life to receive your healing miracle. As you take your spiritual healing prescription (laid out in the next chapter), you will come back to these assessments to tangibly see what your progress has been.

Score each question based on frequency as follows:

Daily = Score 5

3–5 Times Per Week = Score 4

1–2 Times Per Week = Score 3

1–3 Times Per Month = Score 2

Never = Score 0

My Growth Assessment	Score
1) How often do you spend time reading God's word regarding healing (Scriptures or healing accounts)?	
2) How often do you pray regarding healing?	
3) How often do you follow biblical teachings on healing (online sermons, books, studies, etc.)?	
4) How often do you speak God's promises regarding your healing over yourself?	
5) How often do you find yourself casting doubtful thoughts down and replacing them with God's word?	
6) How often do you have conversations with others regarding your expectation of healing?	
7) How often do you thank and praise God regarding the fact that you are healed?	
8) How often do you go to church and other Christian gatherings to feed your faith?	
9) How often do you spend time listening for God's voice for wisdom about your healing?	
10) How often do you sit and visualize yourself already healed?	

Use the above score ratings for the following questions, *but put a minus before the score.*	
1) How often are you researching the sickness online or by other means?	
2) How often do you have anxious or depressed thoughts in relation to the sickness *without* challenging those thoughts with God's word?	
3) How often are you rehearsing the negative issues surrounding the sickness with others?	
4) How often do you experience physical symptoms?	
5) How often are you getting into arguments and strife with others?	
6) Are you angry at anyone or speaking negatively about them? (Yes "-5"/No "0")	
7) Is the sickness one you can see with your eyes? (Yes "-5"/No "0")	
8) Does the sickness typically cause death? (Yes "-5"/No "0")	
9) How likely will natural medicine *cure* it? (Likely "0," Possibly "-3," Unlikely "-5")	
10) Have you had the sickness less than a year? (Yes "-2"/No "-5")	
Box A: Add all *positive* numbers together.	
Box B: Add all *negative* numbers together. (Do not put a minus in this box, just a total.)	
TOTAL SCORE (Box A – Box B):	

There are many items we could put on this assessment, but the general way you think and what you are meditating on each day is a good way to get a snapshot of what your faith level will be.

The second set of questions have a negative scoring to help you see what impact these negative habits are having on your faith and how much unbelief you are sowing into your heart that you have to get rid of. Again, some things listed are out of your control, but you still need to be aware that they exist so you can focus on feeding more faith builders in to counteract their effect on your spirit. The "faith builders" cause you to *function* from a place of faith from your spirit.

The goal is to have high scores on the first set of questions (faith builders) while having as close to a score of 0 as possible on the second set of questions (unbelief builders). That is as far as I am going to go with giving a goal score here because, as I said before, this is not a works thing, and it is not exact. Sometimes certain things will settle in your heart more than they will someone else's, and vice versa, so it is hard to be more concrete than we are. However, there is no question that we need to press as hard as we can toward the goal mentioned.

An important lesson you gain by looking at this concept on the scoring chart is how unbelief counteracts your faith actions and why it is so important to not only put the right things in but to avoid the wrong things as well!

Now let's look at it with a tangible scenario, seeing the natural cause and effect along with the spiritual cause and effect of a healing miracle in parallel.

Natural Need: Weight Loss
Natural Laws Required: Proper Diet and Exercise
Counteraction to Natural Remedy: Improper Diet, Little to No Exercise, etc.

Spiritual Need: Healing Miracle
Spiritual Laws Required: Proper Use/Release of Faith
Counteraction to Spiritual Remedy: Unbelief

Okay, now watch this closely . . .

Weight Loss:

Let's say you do the right thing by eating proper meals each day and going for a daily jog. The change begins; you are applying what is necessary according to the law that governs weight loss to achieve it.

Healing Miracle:

Let's say you start feeding God's word about healing into your spirit and start some faith-building exercises and habits. The change begins, and faith starts moving the healing from the spiritual realm (where the healing already exists) to the natural realm to achieve the *physical* manifestation (remember the diagram in how a healing miracle happens).

So, how important is it to *also* avoid the things that oppose your goal? Let's add them to the mix and see what happens to the equation.

Weight Loss:

You are doing the other things mentioned correctly, according to the natural law to achieve weight loss, but now you add in things that are counteractions to those laws. Now let's say that even though you eat healthy meals all day and are jogging, you start secretly adding in all kinds of junk food and desserts. You may make excuses for it, telling yourself at least you're eating healthier meals and you're also exercising (which you weren't doing before). However, no matter what you tell yourself, you will see the impact those actions have on your goal. And it doesn't matter if you don't believe that will happen, the law will still work the way it works whether you like it or not. While you are still putting right laws in motion, you are putting counteractions in motion against them, and it absolutely affects the progress (it slows it or cancels it out altogether).

Healing Miracle:

You are doing the other things mentioned correctly, according to the laws of healing to see your healing miracle, but now you start adding in some of the things that bring unbelief. It will counteract the faith actions you are taking, and it will affect the progress (the same way the natural example does). It will cancel out your faith completely, or greatly hinder its effectiveness. Here it doesn't matter if you believe it will happen that way or not either, the laws of healing will still operate the way they operate.

After looking at this in this way, it is hard to miss that it is just as imperative to avoid all the things that sow doubt and unbelief in as it is to feed your faith. Stop speaking doubt and unbelief. If the Bible tells you to cast down every thought that exalts itself against God's word and truth (thoughts that say you aren't healed), you see how important it is to take the time to do it! And so on, and so on.

Remember, healing is governed by the laws of healing. They don't work differently for some than they do for others or differently at different times. They work the same way for everyone all the time, and that is what makes them laws. The promises of God are sure, but they don't just fall out of the sky.

My Spiritual Healing Prescription

You apply God's laws on healing as you would a natural prescription. We've already talked so much about the laws of healing and what their effects are. Now we are going to go further with the knowledge we have gained. We would call the things God tells us to sow into our spirit the actual medication. In this chapter, we are talking about the *doing* part, which is the application or implementation. It is *taking the medicine*. If you don't take God's medicine and follow the instructions for the medication, you won't see the results of the medicine. If the doctor told you to take antibiotics three times a day for five days to kill an infection, and you only took it for the first two days, how likely would it be that the infection would be gone?

God's word is surer than any doctor's advice or wisdom could ever be. You have to prioritize and act on what God says as though he is God and he knows what he is talking about! While God is the Great Physician, you have a responsibility as his child (and the patient) to follow his instructions to receive healing.

Dosage

The dosage each Christian needs will be different. It

will vary based on what your spiritual habits have been to date, as well as the severity of the ailment you are dealing with. If you already have a lot of knowledge regarding the healing laws of God and have been sowing those truths on a regular basis in your walk with the Lord, you may only add a few items from the prescription list to what you are already doing.

If this is all new to you, or if you have been diagnosed with a serious disease or are in the advanced stages of a disease, it would benefit you greatly to *immerse* yourself fully in God's medicine.

The *Healing Rx* is geared toward total immersion for faster spiritual growth and results. If you don't feel you need to hyper focus in this manner, scale back to what you feel is best. However, remember that faith comes by hearing. You must be consistently feeding your spirit God's truth and starving out everything contrary to what he says to move in a forward direction spiritually. In the spirit you are never idle, you are either moving forward or backward.

My Healing Rx

Take this Rx daily, 3x per day. During times of struggle, up the dosage or try to find a full day or even a couple of days you can spend with the Lord without distraction of obligations or people, and feed your spirit with these supernatural medicines.

You probably will not do every item on the list each day. *The goal is to spend as much time as you can and to set aside time a few times a day (every day) to take this spiritual medicine.* If you get off track, don't get overwhelmed, just start fresh, and remember God's word works every time!

Be sure to incorporate reading actual healing Scriptures out loud along with the faith declarations daily. These are extremely important.

❖ **Check your heart every day!** If you are upset with anyone, forgive them right then. Let go of anger. Ignore all negative feelings contrary to the fruit of the spirit. If you are depressed or feel doubt, start your day with a simple prayer:

Father, I thank you that your covenant promise of healing is sure, and you have healed me. My feelings are not the truth, your word is the truth. I ignore and refuse all feelings of anger, doubt, unbelief, depression, and fear. I release any person I have held offense against, and I forgive them right now. It doesn't matter what it looks like or how I feel today, your word says I am healed; therefore, I am healed, and that settles it.

❖ **Keep your eyes on Jesus, not your sickness.** Remember when we talked about how Peter experienced a miracle by walking on the water? It was when he took his eyes off Jesus and put them on the circumstances that he "stepped out" of faith and the realm of miracles. It wasn't because he looked at the circumstances, it was because looking at the circumstances brought doubt and unbelief. Keep your focus on God's mighty power and the covenant promises, no matter what you see in the natural. If it worked for Peter (when he did it right), it will work for you if you keep your eyes on Jesus.

❖ **Read healing Scriptures out loud over yourself.** Personalize the Scriptures, inserting "me" or your name when you read them. Many Scriptures are included in this book in other chapters. Highlight the ones that really speak to you. If you have a voice recorder, record yourself reading several of the Scriptures and then listen to that recording several times a day while you read along out loud.

❖ **Pray for your healing!** You will find prayers in this book that you can use to help you. Pray in tongues daily regarding your healing!

❖ **Read the faith declarations in this book.** You can customize this or write your own.

❖ **Cast down every thought contrary to God's word that says you're healed.** Be mindful all day of the thoughts you have and any fear that comes to you. You cast those lying thoughts down by replacing them with what God says. You can simply say, "No, that's a lie. God's word says I am healed, and his healing power is working in my body right now." You can also pull out healing Scriptures or the faith declarations and read them out loud when you need to for this.

❖ **Fast from/avoid all negative conversations, and refrain from looking up doom and gloom information regarding your condition.** Do not engage in this at all!

❖ **Repent of any negative words you speak regarding your condition, and then thank God that his word is true and it is manifesting healing in your body right now!**

❖ **Spend time praising and worshiping God.** Find songs that talk about how mighty and faithful God is, and thank God for healing you.

❖ **Read books, blog posts, and everything you can find online regarding God's healing.** Be sure you only follow teachings that are in line with the word of God. Anything that teaches healing contrary to what the word says, stop giving it attention *immediately*.

❖ **Find testimonies of other people who received God's supernatural healing.** Look for books or search online to find these accounts. Blog articles, videos, whatever you can find. Be building your faith with this constantly!

❖ **Document your progress, and read back over it regularly.** Even small improvements and changes in your symptoms are victories! Document these things, and thank God for them. Constantly go back and read about your progress to build your faith.

❖ **Pick some of the other faith-building exercises in this book and do them!** You can find a list of more exercises in the Healing Tools section. If you think of other exercises on your own, do those too!

❖ **Go to healing meetings!** Search for healing meetings being held by trustworthy ministries who teach God's truths about healing, and go. When you go to these meetings, expect to receive from God!

❖ **Form or join a healing support group.** It is imperative that those you team up with are faith-filled believers! You can search for an online group that already exists, or you can reach out to others you know who are dealing with a sickness and form your own group (remember, only with faith-filled believers). In your group, you can all use this book and do the Healing Rx together! Meet together and study healing, pray, encourage one another, keep up with each other's progress, and watch God's word come to pass!

❖ **Read the Cases of Healing chapter in this book frequently.** Study each case of healing that occurred during Jesus's ministry yourself, and listen for the Holy Spirit to speak to you. Meditate on Jesus's instructions as he ministered healing to others.

❖ **Take communion.** This is powerful, and Jesus told us to do it. When you take communion, remind yourself of the covenant you have in Jesus and how he bore all your sicknesses.

Quick Reference – Healing Rx

Here is a short summary list of the things discussed in this chapter that you can copy and keep with you daily.

DAILY:
1) Check your heart! (Love and Forgiveness)
2) Keep your eyes on Jesus, not the circumstances.
3) Don't be moved by what you see or feel.
4) Read healing Scriptures out loud, 3x day.
5) Read faith declarations out loud, 3x day.
6) Document answered prayers & improvement.
7) Don't give attention to anything that sows doubt.
8) Be mindful of and cast down wrong thoughts.
9) Guard your mouth, only speak God's truth.
10) Pray and praise God for your healing.
ADD DAILY AS ABLE:
1) Watch/listen to testimonies of others healed.
2) Watch/listen to/read teachings on healing.
3) Interact with your healing group.
4) Add a faith-building exercise on days you can.
5) Reread The Laws of Healing, and walk in line with them.
6) Reread Things That Block Healing to remove any that exist.
7) Take Communion often, consider fasting.
Retake assessments periodically to see progress.

I Still Haven't Seen My Miracle, Now What?

When Jesus went with Jairus (one of the rulers of the synagogue) to go heal his daughter who was on the brink of death, along the way a woman with an issue of blood interrupted Jesus, and she was healed. However, while this was going on, someone from Jairus's house came and told him his daughter was dead. Then the Bible says in Mark 5:36: "As soon as Jesus heard the word that was spoken, he saith unto the ruler of the synagogue, Be not afraid, only believe."

It is very important for us to heed what Jesus said in the face of every bad report we get and while we are engaged in the fight of faith in the face of circumstances, reports, or symptoms that don't line up with God's word of healing. This was how Jesus approached the situation. Jesus knew it was *vital* for Jairus to stay in faith to see the miracle he needed, even when the situation looked worse (or impossible)!

This is the very first thing we need to do when fear or doubt tries to creep in. *Stop the fear, and only believe God.* Remember, God is bound by his word, and he is faithful. It is not our job to *make* the miracle happen, that is on God's shoulders. Our job is to believe him regardless of the circumstances and to follow the laws of healing he has shown us. When the pressure comes

130

on and starts getting heavy, we must put our focus back on God, not the things that are pressuring us.

God never says no when we ask or stand for something he has promised in his word to believers. *NEVER.* God cannot lie, he is *bound* by his word. If God promised healing in his word (and he did), *you can have it, and he will never say no to you concerning that request.* It doesn't matter how impossible it seems; your circumstance is not greater than God's ability! Let's remind ourselves of God's word to us:

"For I am the LORD that healeth thee" (Exodus 15:26).

"For I will restore health unto thee, and I will heal thee of thy wounds, saith the LORD" (Jeremiah 30:17).

"For I am the LORD, I change not" (Malachi 3:6).

"God is not a man, that he should lie; neither the son of man, that he should repent: hath he said, and shall he not do it? or hath he spoken, and shall he not make it good?" (Numbers 23:19)

"Then said the LORD unto me, Thou hast well seen: for I will hasten my word to perform it" (Jeremiah 1:12).

(This means, "for I am watching over my word to *perform it*.")

"So shall my word be that goeth forth out of my mouth: it shall not return unto me void, but it shall accomplish that which I please, and it shall prosper in the thing whereto I sent it" (Isaiah 55:11).

"My covenant will I not break, nor alter the thing that is gone out of my lips" (Psalm 89:34).

God is serious when it comes to his word, he is not playing around. Whatever he says, it is *sure*. These Scriptures are God saying to us that he will heal us (he already has), he does not change, he does not lie, and he watches over his word to perform it and bring it to pass. We may not realize this, but the truth is that when we don't take God at his word, we are calling God a *liar*. Now, that is a real eye-opener! Can you imagine having this conversation with God?

"My child, I am God, and I am your Father. I have the power to heal you, and I will do it because I love you and I promised I would, so don't be afraid. You have my word, and I will not break it."

"I'm sorry, God, I just don't believe that. Things look too bad, and I haven't seen it yet, so what you said must be a lie."

When you think about it like that, it really makes you stop in your tracks! That is *exactly* what we are saying to God when we worry and doubt him! If you find yourself discouraged or feeling afraid, it is time to look back at the daily spiritual healing Rx found in this book.

It is possible you will find that you are not immersing yourself in God's word as we have been instructed to do, and that simple correction will get you back on the right track. If you have been immersing yourself in God's word and using the tools listed to walk out your healing, sometimes what you are experiencing is just opposition from the enemy. This is not uncommon!

You may notice that over the last few days or weeks there have been situations where you have had the opportunity to get frustrated or get into strife with family or friends. Maybe one thing after another has come up, you aren't resting, and you are frustrated and "testy." Possibly you have gone in for a follow-up and have received even worse news from your doctor. Perhaps you are experiencing different or more troubling symptoms in relation to the ailment you have been dealing with. If you feel like you have been hitting a wall, or the pressure is coming on from different angles, don't be discouraged! You are right where you are supposed to be.

You have to trust that you are on the right path. God gave us the answers in his word, and he is faithful! It is normal to experience opposition from the enemy, and he will turn up the heat as best he can to get you to think that God's word is a lie. That is when you press in even harder!

If this is happening to you, first settle in your heart that you are absolutely on the right track and right where you need to be. Shake off the pressure for just what it is: the Bible said persecution comes for the word's sake. It comes to try to get you off the word of God. If you keep standing on the word, you will see the promises of God! If you still struggle to get into a place of peace and faith, then increase the time you are spending on your daily spiritual healing Rx.

Again, you need to understand that it is common to face opposition when you are walking things out in faith to see your miracle. When you recognize that is all it is, it is much easier to move forward and not allow it to control your focus.

Don't let circumstances, symptoms, people's opinions, doctor's reports, or anything else dominate your focus. Let God's word be your single target, and meditate on his word alone!

Look at Daniel's experience. On two separate occasions he prayed for an answer from the Lord, and the manifestation happened two different ways. The first account begins in Daniel 9:1. When Daniel was praying, the angel Gabriel came with the answer, and it said: "At the beginning of thy supplications the commandment came forth, and I am come to shew thee" (Daniel 9:23).

Here we see that God gave the command (answer) immediately when Daniel prayed, and in this case the answer manifested immediately to Daniel as the angel came to him while he was still praying. Now let's look at the second time he asked God for an answer in Daniel 10. Daniel says in this account that for three full weeks he was fasting and praying for the answer he was awaiting. The angel finally came after three weeks and this is what they said:

Then said he unto me, Fear not, Daniel: for from the first day that thou didst set thine heart to understand, and to chasten thyself before thy God, thy words were heard, and I am come for thy words. But the prince of the kingdom of Persia withstood me one and twenty days. (Daniel 10:12–13)

In this instance, it is important to note that the answer was also given by God immediately when Daniel prayed! He didn't see the manifestation immediately, but it was already on its way! This shows us that sometimes there is spiritual opposition that can delay things that we have prayed for. What would have happened if Daniel had given up?! Notice that the angel said, "I am come for *thy words*"! It is imperative to listen to God when he tells us there is power in the words we speak, and to continue to only speak the truth of God's word regarding our healing, no matter what it looks like. The Bible says we walk by faith, and not by sight! Do not give up! Keep pressing in, and expect to see your healing manifest because you *are* healed.

Whether the manifestation comes while you are praying, or it comes in three weeks, it will come! God always answers us immediately when we pray according to his will, and his will is to heal us. He already provided your healing when Jesus paid for it in full, and you *were healed* the moment you prayed in faith to receive it. God's word *never fails*.

Meet the Healer

Meeting the Healer himself is an experience like no other. If you are already a Christian, I invite you to go deeper. If you are not, ask him to be Lord of your life today: you don't know what you are missing! Imagine this with me . . .

God Almighty himself. The one who spoke the world into existence, who tells the water of the seas how far they can go and what their boundaries are. Who commands the lightning. Who breathed breath into dust and formed life and the human spirit. Who designed the human body to function with such complexity and perfection. Who knew you before you were born.

The one who knows everything, from the beginning to the end. He knew the entire future before it even began. The angels worship him without ceasing. He rules from his majestic throne and all things bend to his command. The world exists because he made it so. The stars hang in the sky at his desire.

He holds all power, and no power or authority is higher. He knows the number of hairs on your head every second of every day. He knows the root of every problem, he knows every solution, and he has the power to carry it out.

The Bible says that one day every knee shall bow before him and that every tongue will confess that Jesus Christ is Lord.

He is all consuming, his vastness is beyond comprehension. His thoughts are higher than our thoughts. His ways are perfect. And yet . . .

He loves us, and when we accept what Jesus did for us, we become his family. Not his servants, not just his created beings, we are his children. As his children, we have access to everything that he has. Everything. All that he owns, all his power. He made a blood covenant through Jesus with us.

We couldn't make God do anything at all if he did not desire it to be so. We wouldn't see any change in the midst of our misery if God did not grant it. The beautiful thing is that *he chose* to be bound to us, and *he chose* to make his covenant with us. He knew we could never live up to perfection or earn any of these promises he has given to us, and yet he loved us so much he gave us the abundant life in his word.

That is why the Scriptures say in 1 John 4:19, "We love him, because he first loved us." When you begin to get a revelation of all the things God has already done and promised you that you could never be good enough to attain, you *can't help* but love him. The revelation of those things will bring you to your knees in gratitude and awe. The Great King. The Great "I am." The Author of the Universe. And yet we march right up to the throne as his kids and through inheritance have access to it *all*.

God told us he doesn't want us begging him, he wants us to expect to receive all that he has promised us as his children and come boldly before him and receive it. A servant is sheepish, a servant makes their case *hoping*. A child makes their case *expecting*. A child goes in and takes what they need when their parent has told them they can have it, with a grateful heart, but they *take it!*

You are the one that determines how you go to the Father, what kind of relationship you have with him. He can tell you that you are his child, but if you decide to approach him as a servant, that is *your* choice. This is how your Father wants you to have a relationship with him: When you need something God has promised, such as healing, you see yourself marching right up to his throne room before him and getting it. You don't come in crawling. You don't come in begging. You don't even knock, you just walk right in. Can you imagine this? When you pray, close your eyes and see your Father's throne room. And march up to it! Not because you're greater than God, but because he told you to, and you don't insult his gift by behaving like a servant and telling God you are not willing to be his child.

He wanted a family; he wanted you! Will you deprive him of that? Would you want your children running around not taking you at your word when you tell them something? Would you want your children doubting your faithfulness to do what you said you would do? Not expecting God to honor his word or approaching him as though he did not make you his child is an insult to his goodness, integrity, and his power to do so. Have you ever thought about that? "Let us therefore come boldly unto the throne of grace, that we may obtain mercy, and find grace to help in time of need" (Hebrews 4:16).

God is the ruler of all things, the God of all that is, and it is time we recognize how mighty he is and approach him as our Father. That is where the freedom is to receive. We don't live with the thought that maybe he will; we live with the expectation that he is more than able, and he will do it!

The Author of Faith

We have spent so much time looking at faith, what it is, how it works, and how to function in it. The bottom line is that we don't get the promises without God. Without him, we would have no promises. We don't get healing without the Healer.

So, with all that we have covered about faith, the final point is this: God is the author of our faith. It is so important that we understand this. Our faith will function when we realize who God is, and what his covenant is with us. *How do you have faith in a promise*

if you don't have confidence in the one who made it?
Pressing into a deeper relationship with God and
spending more time in his presence brings this
confidence. And that confidence puts our faith into
overdrive!

"And this is the confidence that we have in him, that,
if we ask any thing according to his will, he heareth us:
And if we know that he hear us, whatsoever we ask, we
know that we have the petitions that we desired of him"
(1 John 5:14–15).

If we put our eyes on who God is, and who he is to
us, we will find that our confidence (faith) becomes sure
for the things we are believing for! In Mark 11 we see
Jesus giving us the basic outline of receiving a miracle,
and we have covered that in this book, but let's look
again it.

And Jesus answering saith unto them, Have faith in
God. For verily I say unto you, That whosoever shall
say unto this mountain, Be thou removed, and be
thou cast into the sea; and shall not doubt in his
heart, but shall believe that those things which he
saith shall come to pass; he shall have whatsoever
he saith. Therefore I say unto you, What things
soever ye desire, when ye pray, believe that ye

receive them, and ye shall have them. (Mark 11:22–24)

The very first thing Jesus said is "Have faith in God." That is where the very heart of our faith rests, focused on God himself. Faith comes by hearing, but what do we have faith *in* when faith comes? In God! And not only do we have faith in God, but we have faith in God's love for us. *Of course* you are healed, because God loves you.

"He that spared not his own Son, but delivered him up for us all, how shall he not with him also freely give us all things?" (Romans 8:32)

Meditating on the love God has for you and being in his presence changes *everything*. This verse says that he didn't even spare his own son when it came to you, and that being the case, why would you *ever* doubt he would *freely* heal you? Say this prayer of salvation and receive what God has made available to you right now:

Jesus, I believe you died on the cross for my sins and that you were raised from the dead. I ask you to come into my heart and be Lord in my life. I repent of my sins, and I receive your forgiveness right now. I come to you just as I am, and I give my life to you. Change me for your glory. In the name of Jesus I pray, amen.

Healing Tools

This section includes many tools that will help you position yourself for healing and help build your faith. Refer back to this section regularly as you immerse yourself in the word of God!

Faith-Building Exercises

These are ideas you can use to build your faith. Incorporating some of these exercises into your daily spiritual healing Rx are extremely helpful in keeping your heart and mind focused on your healing and helping you position yourself to receive healing according to the laws of healing we see in the word.

You do not have to do every exercise suggested; pick the ones that fit you!

* ❖ **Write out your own faith declarations.** Directing your mind to think and focus on God's truths to write out your own statements causes you to meditate on God's word. You can use the examples of the faith declarations in this book to get ideas. This exercise is just taking time to write out your own beliefs and thoughts regarding your healing.

* ❖ **Write your prayers.** This is similar to the first suggestion, but again, there is something about writing things down. These exercises are great, especially on days where you are feeling discouraged. Just get a good cup of tea or coffee, sit somewhere quiet, and get your mind and heart moving with faith!

* **Write out your "standing" (or grounds) for your healing.** In a court case, a person's standing is based on the laws that support that person's ability to make the request they are making in the case. We are receiving our healing based on God's promises according to his laws. What is it that makes your healing sure? Why is it granted to you? Put your mind on those things, and write them down.

* **Journal about your healing manifestation.** Don't journal about the negative things you see right now. This is to help you begin to meditate on and see yourself healed! What will change when your healing manifests? What will you do that you couldn't do before? Where will you go? How will your life be different? Write out all these things in the *present tense*. You are already healed!

* **Draw yourself healed.** If you like to draw, spend time drawing yourself healed and doing different things and going places you were not able to go to before.

* **Make a vision board.** Include pictures of yourself healthy, include pictures of all the things

you will be doing, places you will be going, etc. when your healing manifests.

❖ **Practice meditation and visualization.** Set aside quiet time when you will not be interrupted. Get comfortable, close your eyes, and see yourself healed and doing all the things that you will be doing when your healing manifests. Sometimes it helps to narrate out loud what you are visualizing with your eyes closed. Do all this as though it is present tense.

❖ **Answered prayers list.** Take time to think back on and write down all the prayers God has already answered in your life, big and small! Build on this list going forward. Incorporate this list as part of your daily spiritual healing Rx, and go back and reflect on it often. When you are reading these answered prayers, praise God for his faithfulness!

❖ **Write out your testimony of healing!** Think about what you would send to someone who is dealing with what you have been dealing with. What would you say to them after your healing manifests to tell them about the miracle you received? Do this as though the healing has already manifested!

❖ **Testify of the healing power of God.** If you were to write a blog post or a letter to a good friend dealing with sickness, what would you write to the reader to encourage them about God's promise to heal them? How would you encourage them? What would you tell them to do and not to do?

❖ **Begin planning your future.** If you have been told there is no cure for your condition, do not accept that. If your diagnosis is not that extreme, you still need to spend time meditating on this. Start spending time putting your mind on what you plan to do with your life in the future! If it is starting a business, begin to pray about that, and research how that would come together. If it is going back to school, start looking at where you would go, what classes you would take, how to get enrolled, etc. The point of this exercise is to just move forward in your mind and heart with your future, and not to consider any thoughts or reports that hinder you from fulfilling God's purpose in your life. It's about seeing yourself living out a long and blessed life on this earth, completely whole!

You will notice God's word is incorporated into the prayers here. Also, when it comes to praying for something God has already provided for and promised us in his word, we don't *continue* to "ask" for it. In fact, we don't have to ask for healing at all, we just receive it. And if we "believed we received it when we prayed," like Jesus instructed us to do in Mark 11 where he taught on miracles, then any praying done after our first prayer when we received it should sound like *we already have it.*

There is no set-in-stone prayer when it comes to healing; these are just to help you if you would like to use them, and there is extreme power in them.

Initial Prayer – Receiving Your Healing

Father, I come before you based on your covenant promises of healing. I believe that Jesus paid for my healing in full by the stripes he took on his back, and I believe it is always your will to heal. I believe you made healing available to me through what Jesus did on my behalf, and by faith I receive healing in my body right now. _____ (say the disease/diagnosis) is not more powerful than you or your word, and right now I command _____ (say the disease/diagnosis) to be removed from me in Jesus's name. _____ (say the disease/diagnosis) you have no part in me, and you have no authority to stay in my body.

Right this minute, I am totally whole, and I enforce the word of God against you. You have no choice now but to obey the word of God and go from my body right now. I speak to _____ (list any symptoms such as pain, inflammation, nausea, fever, dizziness, etc.), and I command you to go from my body right now in Jesus's name. I deny the right of all sickness and disease and any symptoms caused by them to exist in my body. You are trespassing, and you must leave right now.

I refuse all doubt and unbelief. It doesn't matter what it looks like or how I feel, I walk by faith and not by sight, and right now as I am praying, God's supernatural healing power is working in my body. I trust you, Father, and I take you at your word. Your word is final authority in my life, and I thank you for healing me. Your word says you will restore health unto me and heal me of all my wounds. Your word says you are the Lord that heals me. Your word says you will take all sickness away from the midst of me. Your word says Jesus bore my sickness; therefore, I am free from it. Sickness is under the curse, and I have been redeemed from the curse. Thank you, Lord, that you manifest yourself to me. I will see my healing manifest, and on the authority I have in the name of Jesus, I receive my healing, and I am healed right now. Amen.

Prayers – When Waiting for Healing to Manifest

Thank you, Father, that your word is sure. The Bible says your word is tried, and it is a shield to me who has put my trust in you. Your word is absolutely certain, and you have made a blood covenant with me through what Jesus did when he bore my sicknesses at the cross to heal me. Your word cannot fail. You cannot fail. Your word will surely come to pass in my life, and I will see my complete and total healing manifest. I am already healed! I believe it, and I refuse to doubt! I refuse all thoughts and feelings to the contrary of your healing promises, they are lies, and your word is truth. Thank you for healing me, Father!

• • • •

I'm so excited, Father, that I am healed! I know I am already healed! I can't wait to testify to others of when my healing physically manifested! To your name be all the glory. Father, I thank you that my healing is a testimony to many others, and many will believe on you through this. You are so faithful and so good. You never withhold any good thing from me, including my healing. I am not begging to be healed, you already promised to heal me before I ever had need of it, and I am already healed. You can't wait to show yourself strong on my behalf, you are not delaying my healing from manifesting. Your word is working in my body right now, and it is producing the fruit of healing miracles right now. Praise your holy name!

Prayer – When Symptoms Are Bad or When Battling Doubt

Father, thank you that my healing was sure and settled when I first prayed. Nothing has changed that truth. Nothing can stop your healing power from manifesting in my body. _____ (say the sickness/disease) cannot stand against your word. It is weak compared to your power. Healing is easy for you, and you are bound by your word to heal me. I refuse every thought that has tried to come in and cause me to doubt.

_____

_____

_____

(List all doubtful thoughts you can think of, and then declare, "That's a lie, and I refuse to believe it." Example: "The thought, 'What if I don't get healed,' that's a lie, and I refuse to believe it. God's word is true, and I am healed. The thought, 'I'm going to die,' that's a lie, and I refuse to believe it. God's word says I will live and not die. His word is true, and I am healed.")

I don't care how I feel, I don't care what my symptoms are, God's word is true, and I am healed. No matter how many doubtful thoughts try to come in, no matter what pressure I feel, God's word is true, and I am healed. I am totally well, and there will be no other outcome. God's word settles it in my life. God's word has manifested healing in my body, and his word is working in me right now, regardless of what it looks like. I believe his Word only, and I am perfectly whole.

It doesn't matter what other people's experiences have been and whether they received their healing or not. If they didn't receive their healing, that is between them and God. I will not rest my faith for my healing on them, I rest it on God and his covenant with me alone. The only thing that matters is God's word and my believing him, I refuse to consider anything else.

Now, body, I command you to line up with the word of God. You are already whole, and you manifest healing right now in the name of Jesus.

Prayer – When Feeling Condemnation

Thank you, Father, that my healing is not based on my works, it is based on the covenant you made with me through what Jesus did on the cross. I repent if I have sinned against you, have not walked in love, or have gotten into doubt or anything else that moves against my healing. Right now, all that is settled, and it cannot hinder me. Your word that says I am healed is producing healing in my body. I refuse all condemnation. Father, I thank you that you love me, that nothing can separate me from your love, and that I just receive your love and your perfect healing.

Faith Declarations

These are quick faith-filled statements you can say when you are combating negative doubtful thoughts to help you stay focused and in faith for your healing. As you declare these things out loud, they will literally bring peace to your soul and give you rest. You can jump around or highlight the ones that speak to your spirit the most. It is good to set time aside regularly as one of your faith exercises to speak these things over yourself. This is just another helpful tool that sows faith and expectation for your miracle into you.

It is also good to have a simple belief declaration committed to memory to use all day and throughout the day when you aren't looking at this list. Here's something short and simple that will work to combat any thought that challenges what God says about your healing or makes you feel fearful: "That is a lie, and I refuse to believe it. God's word of healing is working in me right now, and I am already healed."

Here are more declarations to use:

❖ Father you are the healer. You said to me, "I am the Lord that healeth thee," and I believe you.

❖ I believe I am already healed. Jesus said that if I believe I received my healing when I prayed, then I have it.

❖ Father, you said to me that you will restore health unto me and heal me of all my wounds, and I thank you that my health is restored right now.

❖ It does not matter what it looks like, how I feel, or what I have been told. The only thing that matters is that God said I am healed, and therefore, I am healed. God said it, and that settles it.

❖ No sickness can stay in my body. God's power is greater than any sickness, and no matter how bad it looks or how long it has persisted, the days of sickness and disease in my body are over, and it is already gone!

❖ The thought that I am not healed is a lie. The thought that the word isn't working is a lie. God said he watches over his word to perform it. Right now, he is looking at his words of healing that I have spoken into my body, and his word is manifesting that healing.

❖ God's word works every time. God cannot fail, his word cannot fail, and he cannot lie. I am healed, and I will see the healing miracle manifest in my physical body because I'm already healed.

❖ Jesus purchased my healing: he paid for me to be well. It was paid *in full.* He bore all sickness and disease on my behalf, and I am healed.

❖ I choose to believe God regardless of what anyone else says. God has the final say in my life, and I am healed.

❖ The odds and statistics according to natural medicine do not apply to me. I have been redeemed from the curse, and God's laws of healing *govern* my physical body. I will not be governed by any sickness. I rebuke it and command it to leave in Jesus's name, and I'm already healed.

❖ Every symptom I have been experiencing from sickness leaves right now. I am not sick, I am healed; therefore, no symptoms of sickness can stay either.

- My God is greater than _____ (name the sickness). It has to bow to the name of Jesus, the name that is above every name. _____ (name the sickness) has no other option but to leave my body right now.

- I refuse to reason; I refuse to doubt. I believe only because I have already been made whole. I don't have to understand how it works. My God knows how to bring healing into my body. He is up for the job. He is responsible to heal me according to his word, and he has done it.

- God said he has healed me; therefore, I am healed. There is nothing that can stand against the word of my God. When he says something, everything bends to line up with his word. Sickness is bending to the word of God and is gone from my body because I am completely and totally whole.

- I refuse sickness in my body. I speak to _____ (name the sickness), and I deny your right to exist in me. *You have no place in me.* I remind you that I am a child of God Almighty, and I have been redeemed from the curse. Jesus already defeated you and brought you to nothing. You have no right to exist in me; therefore, I am free of you, and there is no remnant or evidence of you left in my body.

❖ I am full of the peace of God that surpasses all understanding. I have total peace because God promised it to me. I don't worry about any sickness, because God is faithful, and I was already healed. I will see healing manifest in my body because it is a *done deal*, and that truth brings peace to my soul right now.

❖ It is God's job to heal me, and he has done it. Healing is my right and privilege by the covenant God made with me. My healing is guaranteed, and it is already done by the blood of Jesus and the stripes he took on his back.

❖ I expect to see healing manifest in my body because I am healed. Every symptom of sickness is gone. I live every day of my life whole.

❖ There can be no other outcome for me but total wholeness. God's word is certain. Nothing can change the fact and the truth that he has healed me.

❖ I am not afraid that I won't be healed; I cast that thought down. That is not even a possibility because I am already healed, and it is sealed by the blood of Jesus. I am not waiting to get my healing. Right this minute, right where I am, I am already healed.

❖ God loves me. He gave his son to die for me. He watches over me every second of every day. If God has a favorite, it is me. *Of course* he healed me!

❖ God's love for me can never be shaken. There will never come a day that God turns his back on me. He is mine, and I am his, and he has healed me.

❖ I am confident in God's faithfulness and his love for me. God has never failed, and he isn't going to start today. He is *my* Healer, and he healed me!

Healing Scriptures

Psalm 30:2–3

"O Lord my God, I cried unto thee, and thou hast healed me. O Lord, thou hast brought up my soul from the grave: thou hast kept me alive."

John 15:7

"If ye abide in me, and my words abide in you, ye shall ask what ye will, and it shall be done unto you."

Psalm 34:17

"The righteous cry, and the Lord heareth, and delivereth them out of all their troubles."

Psalm 34:19

"Many are the afflictions of the righteous: but the Lord delivereth him out of them all."

Psalm 103:2–5

Bless the Lord, O my soul, and forget not all his benefits: Who forgiveth all thine iniquities; who healeth all thy diseases; Who redeemeth thy life from destruction; who crowneth thee with lovingkindness and tender mercies; Who satisfieth thy mouth with good things; so that thy youth is renewed like the eagle's.

Isaiah 53:4
"Surely he hath borne our griefs, and carried our sorrows."

Isaiah 53:5
"But he was wounded for our transgressions, he was bruised for our iniquities: the chastisement of our peace was upon him; and with his stripes we are healed."

Exodus 12:13
"And the blood shall be to you for a token upon the houses where ye are: and when I see the blood, I will pass over you, and the plague shall not be upon you to destroy you."

Exodus 23:25
"And I will take sickness away from the midst of thee."

Exodus 23:26
"The number of thy days I will fulfill."

Deuteronomy 7:15
"And the LORD will take away from thee all sickness."

Galatians 3:29

"And if ye be Christ's, then are ye Abraham's seed, and heirs according to the promise."

Deuteronomy 33:25

"And as thy days, so shall thy strength be."

Psalm 118:17

"I shall not die, but live, and declare the works of the LORD."

Job 33:24–25

"Then he is gracious unto him, and saith, Deliver him from going down to the pit: I have found a ransom. His flesh shall be fresher than a child's: he shall return to the days of his youth."

Psalm 29:11

"The LORD will give strength unto his people; the LORD will bless his people with peace."

Psalm 41:2

"The LORD will preserve him, and keep him alive; and he shall be blessed upon the earth."

Psalm 41:3

"The LORD will strengthen him upon the bed of languishing."

Psalm 43:5

"Hope in God: for I shall yet praise him, who is the health of my countenance, and my God."

Psalm 91:3

"Surely he shall deliver thee from the snare of the fowler, and from the noisome pestilence."

Psalm 91:5–7

Thou shalt not be afraid for the terror by night; nor for the arrow that flieth by day; Nor for the pestilence that walketh in darkness; nor for the destruction that wasteth at noonday. A thousand shall fall at thy side, and ten thousand at thy right hand; but it shall not come nigh thee.

Psalm 91:10

"There shall no evil befall thee, neither shall any plague come nigh thy dwelling."

Psalm 91:15–16

"He shall call upon me, and I will answer him: I will be with him in trouble; I will deliver him, and honour him. With long life will I satisfy him, and shew him my salvation."

Psalm 107:20

"He sent his word, and healed them, and delivered them from their destructions."

Psalm 138:7

"Though I walk in the midst of trouble, thou wilt revive me."

Psalm 138:8

"The LORD will perfect that which concerneth me."

Psalm 147:3

"He healeth the broken in heart, and bindeth up their wounds."

Proverbs 4:10

"Hear, O my son, and receive my sayings; and the years of thy life shall be many."

Proverbs 3:1–2

"My son, forget not my law; but let thine heart keep my commandments: For length of days, and long life, and peace, shall they add to thee."

Proverbs 4:20–22

"My son, attend to my words; incline thine ear unto my sayings. Let them not depart from thine eyes; keep them in the midst of thine heart. For they are life unto those that find them, and health to all their flesh."

Proverbs 17:22
"A merry heart doeth good like a medicine."

Isaiah 35:4
"Say to them that are of a fearful heart, Be strong, fear not: behold, your God will come with vengeance, even God with a recompense; he will come and save you."

Isaiah 38:16
"So wilt thou recover me, and make me to live."

Isaiah 40:29
"He giveth power to the faint; and to them that have no might he increaseth strength."

Isaiah 40:31
"But they that wait upon the Lord shall renew their strength; they shall mount up with wings as eagles; they shall run, and not be weary; and they shall walk, and not faint."

Isaiah 57:18
"I have seen his ways, and will heal him: I will lead him also, and restore comforts unto him and to his mourners."

Isaiah 57:19

"I create the fruit of the lips; Peace, peace to him that is far off, and to him that is near, saith the LORD; and I will heal him."

Isaiah 58:8a

"Then shall thy light break forth as the morning, and thine health shall spring forth speedily."

Isaiah 58:9

"Then shalt thou call, and the LORD shall answer; thou shalt cry, and he shall say, Here I am."

Jeremiah 17:14

"Heal me, O LORD, and I shall be healed."

Jeremiah 30:17

"For I will restore health unto thee, and I will heal thee of thy wounds, saith the Lord."

Jeremiah 33:6

"Behold, I will bring it health and cure, and I will cure them, and will reveal unto them the abundance of peace and truth."

Ezekiel 34:16

"I will seek that which was lost, and bring again that which was driven away, and will bind up that which was broken, and will strengthen that which was sick."

Ezekiel 37:5

"Behold, I will cause breath to enter into you, and ye shall live."

Ezekiel 37:14

"And shall put my spirit in you, and ye shall live."

Amos 5:6

"Seek the LORD, and ye shall live."

Malachi 4:2

"But unto you that fear my name shall the Sun of righteousness arise with healing in his wings."

Matthew 8:3

"And Jesus put forth his hand, and touched him, saying, I will; be thou clean. And immediately his leprosy was cleansed."

Matthew 8:17

"Himself took our infirmities, and bare our sicknesses."

Matthew 10:7–8

"And as ye go, preach, saying, The kingdom of heaven is at hand. Heal the sick, cleanse the lepers, raise the dead, cast out devils: freely ye have received, freely give."

Matthew 14:14

"And Jesus went forth, and saw a great multitude, and was moved with compassion toward them, and he healed their sick."

Matthew 4:23

"And Jesus went about all Galilee, teaching in their synagogues, and preaching the gospel of the kingdom, and healing all manner of sickness and all manner of disease among the people."

Matthew 9:29–30

"Then touched he their eyes, saying, According to your faith be it unto you. And their eyes were opened."

Matthew 10:1

"And when he had called unto him his twelve disciples, he gave them power against unclean spirits, to cast them out, and to heal all manner of sickness and all manner of disease."

Luke 5:17

"And the power of the Lord was present to heal them."

Luke 9:1–2

"Then he called his twelve disciples together, and gave them power and authority over all devils, and to cure diseases. And he sent them to preach the kingdom of God, and to heal the sick."

Matthew 12:15

"But when Jesus knew it, he withdrew himself from thence: and great multitudes followed him, and he healed them all."

Hebrews 13:8

"Jesus Christ the same yesterday, and to day, and for ever."

Matthew 14:35–36

"And when the men of that place had knowledge of him, they sent out into all that country round about, and brought unto him all that were diseased; And besought him that they might only touch the hem of his garment: and as many as touched were made perfectly whole."

Matthew 15:28

"Then Jesus answered and said unto her, O woman, great is thy faith: be it unto thee even as thou wilt. And her daughter was made whole from that very hour."

Mark 7:37

"And were beyond measure astonished, saying, He hath done all things well: he maketh both the deaf to hear, and the dumb to speak."

Mark 9:23

"Jesus said unto him, If thou canst believe, all things are possible to him that believeth."

Mark 11:22–23

And Jesus answering saith unto them, Have faith in God. For verily I say unto you, That whosoever shall say unto this mountain, Be thou removed, and be thou cast into the sea; and shall not doubt in his heart, but shall believe that those things which he saith shall come to pass; he shall have whatsoever he saith.

Mark 16:18

"They shall lay hands on the sick, and they shall recover."

Luke 9:11

"And he received them, and spake unto them of the kingdom of God, and healed them that had need of healing."

Luke 9:56

"For the Son of man is not come to destroy men's lives, but to save them."

Luke 10:19

"Behold, I give unto you power to tread on serpents and scorpions, and over all the power of the enemy: and nothing shall by any means hurt you."

1 John 4:4

"Ye are of God, little children, and have overcome them: because greater is he that is in you, than he that is in the world."

John 6:33

"For the bread of God is he which cometh down from heaven, and giveth life unto the world."

John 8:36

"If the Son therefore shall make you free, ye shall be free indeed."

John 10:10

"The thief cometh not, but for to steal, and to kill, and to destroy: I am come that they might have life, and that they might have it more abundantly."

John 14:13–14

"And whatsoever ye shall ask in my name, that will I do, that the Father may be glorified in the Son. If ye shall ask any thing in my name, I will do it."

Psalm 55:16–18

"As for me, I will call upon God; and the LORD shall save me. Evening, and morning, and at noon, will I pray, and cry aloud: and he shall hear my voice. He hath delivered my soul in peace from the battle that was against me: for there were many with me."

Psalm 55:22

"Cast thy burden upon the LORD, and he shall sustain thee: he shall never suffer the righteous to be moved."

Psalm 116:8–9

"For thou hast delivered my soul from death, mine eyes from tears, and my feet from falling. I will walk before the LORD in the land of the living."

Joel 2:32

"And it shall come to pass, that whosoever shall call on the name of the LORD shall be delivered."

2 Thessalonians 3:3

"But the Lord is faithful, who shall stablish you, and keep you from evil."

Acts 10:38

"How God anointed Jesus of Nazareth with the Holy Ghost and with power: who went about doing good, and healing all that were oppressed of the devil; for God was with him."

Acts 17:25

"Seeing he giveth to all life, and breath, and all things."

Psalm 145:14

"The LORD upholdeth all that fall, and raiseth up all those that be bowed down."

Isaiah 40:31

"But they that wait upon the LORD shall renew their strength."

Acts 19:11–12

"And God wrought special miracles by the hands of Paul: So that from his body were brought unto the sick handkerchiefs or aprons, and the diseases departed from them."

Romans 8:2

"For the law of the Spirit of life in Christ Jesus hath made me free from the law of sin and death."

Romans 8:11

"But if the Spirit of him that raised up Jesus from the dead dwell in you, he that raised up Christ from the dead shall also quicken your mortal bodies by his Spirit that dwelleth in you."

2 Corinthians 1:10

"Who delivered us from so great a death, and doth deliver: in whom we trust that he will yet deliver us."

Ephesians 6:3

"That it may be well with thee, and thou mayest live long on the earth."

Psalm 4:8

"I will both lay me down in peace, and sleep: for thou, LORD, only makest me dwell in safety."

Colossians 1:13

"Who hath delivered us from the power of darkness, and hath translated us into the kingdom of his dear Son."

2 Timothy 4:18

"And the Lord shall deliver me from every evil work."

Hebrews 12:13

"And make straight paths for your feet, lest that which is lame be turned out of the way; but let it rather be healed."

James 5:14–15

"Is any sick among you? let him call for the elders of the church; and let them pray over him, anointing him with oil in the name of the Lord: And the prayer of faith shall save the sick, and the Lord shall raise him up."

James 5:16

"Confess your faults one to another, and pray one for another, that ye may be healed. The effectual fervent prayer of a righteous man availeth much."

1 Peter 2:24

"Who his own self bare our sins in his own body on the tree, that we, being dead to sins, should live unto righteousness: by whose stripes ye were healed."

2 Peter 1:3

"According as his divine power hath given unto us all things that pertain unto life and godliness."

Proverbs 18:21

"Death and life are in the power of the tongue."

Proverbs 3:23

"Then shalt thou walk in thy way safely, and thy foot shall not stumble."

Revelation 22:17

"And whosoever will, let him take the water of life freely."

1 John 3:8

"For this purpose the Son of God was manifested, that he might destroy the works of the devil."

3 John 2:2

"Beloved, I wish above all things that thou mayest prosper and be in health, even as thy soul prospereth."

Psalm 23:1–6

> The LORD is my shepherd; I shall not want. He maketh me to lie down in green pastures: he leadeth me beside the still waters. He restoreth my soul: he leadeth me in the paths of righteousness for his name's sake. Yea, though I walk through the valley of the shadow of death, I will fear no evil: for thou art with me; thy rod and thy staff they comfort me. Thou preparest a table before me in the presence of mine enemies: thou anointest my head with oil; my cup runneth over. Surely goodness and mercy shall

follow me all the days of my life: and I will dwell in the house of the LORD for ever.

In this chapter we will look at every account in Jesus's ministry where healing occurred. First, I am going to outline some of the overall findings based on those cases, and you can see their validity as you read through each case. Most of these truths have already been touched on earlier in the book, but this is a good list to review continually! Especially if you find yourself standing in faith while you wait for your healing to manifest. It will build your faith as you keep your eyes on God's truth concerning your healing.

If the account of the healing is recorded in more than one book in the Bible, I have compiled each account together to make it easier to follow everything about that healing that has been recorded for us. I have also added notes that you may find helpful or interesting regarding each case.

Healing Points in Summary

1. It is God's will to heal, all the time, every time. God *wants* to heal every person.

2. God never says no to healing. Jesus *never* said no when someone approached him for healing. He healed in every one of those instances.

3. Healing *always comes* when we receive it by faith. Jesus healed even when people didn't have "faith that takes it," but in those situations his faith was used. *Someone* must have faith!

4. Jesus bore every sickness and disease when he died on the cross, took the stripes on his back for healing, and said "It is finished." He gave his life for the redemption of sin, but he took the stripes for healing.

5. It doesn't matter how old you are, you don't have to expect to be sick or have diseases just because you're older. (Again, every person who sought healing was healed. There were no accounts that someone did not get healed because of their age.)

6. The *only* reason Scripture shows people did *not* get healed in Jesus's ministry was because of unbelief.

7. God does not pick and choose who gets healed. Anyone who wants to be healed and reaches out

to God according to the laws of healing can have it.

8. God does not put sickness on any person, ever. In the new testament it says that Jesus came that we may have life and have it more abundantly. The Bible also says that the devil comes to kill, steal, and destroy. It says God poured out all his wrath (punishment) on Jesus.

9. Christians have God's power to heal within them. *Every* Christian, not just those with the gift of healing.

10. *Only* Christians have the authority to use the name of Jesus and minister healing.

11. Christians are *commanded* to go out and heal the sick.

12. Healing is a blood covenant promise, backed by the blood of Jesus. God cut covenant with us.

13. God cannot lie: he is bound by and must honor his word.

14. You can receive healing *how* you want to if you can have faith for it.

15. Different methods of supernatural healing:
    1. God heals when he chooses (intervenes on his own at his discretion).
    2. God heals through someone with a healing gift.
    3. God will heal others based on the faith of a Christian that is praying for them.
    4. God heals us based on our own faith to receive.

16. God is not trying to hide how healing works from us!! He is not going to withhold knowledge and understanding regarding healing! Scriptures tell us that anyone who asks receives, and anyone who lacks wisdom let him ask. Remember, he commanded us to do it; therefore, he will not hide things from us.

17. Healing and miracles are for today. Jesus told the disciples what their purpose was: to go out and preach the gospel to every creature and to heal the sick, raise the dead, cast out devils, etc. Then he told them to teach other believers to do likewise. Nowhere in the word does it say this mandate changed. The Bible says God is the same yesterday, today, and forever.

18. When Jesus ministered, it was always simple. Usually he spoke very few words when he healed the sick. He didn't have to pray over them for hours. I'm not saying we are "doing it wrong" when we pray more than a few words. It is okay to pray longer prayers. A lot of times that is more for us: to get our heart's desires out and get our spiritual eyes on the finished outcome, as well as to build our faith while we are praying to release it for the healing. It can also build the faith of the person we are ministering to as they hear our prayers.

19. You will notice in the different accounts when Jesus specifically said that a person was healed because of their faith. He did that on purpose to let us know that is how *that* person got their miracle.

20. In some cases, demons were the reason for the sickness and caused the symptoms of the sickness. Jesus had to cast them out for the person to be healed. If that was true then, there will be cases where it is true now. Notice casting demons out was not some long fight, or from the reciting of prayers. They go out when we command them to leave.

As you read through the different cases of healing, keep in mind that Jesus did everything with a calculated and specific purpose. He never did anything that didn't matter. He never said anything that didn't matter. Look at each account with that mindset to see what God is trying to relay to you with his word.

Healing Accounts

Account 1: A Multitude Is Healed
Matthew 4:23–24, Mark 1:39, Luke 4:44

Matthew:

> And Jesus went about all Galilee, teaching in their synagogues, and preaching the gospel of the kingdom, and healing all manner of sickness and all manner of disease among the people. And his fame went throughout all Syria: and they brought unto him all sick people that were taken with divers diseases and torments, and those which were possessed with devils, and those which were lunatick, and those that had the palsy; and he healed them.

Mark:

"And he preached in their synagogues throughout all Galilee, and cast out devils."

Luke:

"And he preached in the synagogues of Galilee."

- ❖ Jesus healed *all* manner of sickness and disease.
- ❖ Many people were healed, and it does not note anyone who was not healed.
- ❖ This is Jesus's ministry in a snapshot: he went about preaching, healing the sick, and casting out devils.

Account 2: A Leper Is Healed
Matthew 8:2–4, Mark 1:40–45, Luke 5:12–15

Matthew:

And, behold, there came a leper and worshipped him, saying, Lord, if thou wilt, thou canst make me clean. And Jesus put forth his hand, and touched him, saying, I will; be thou clean. And immediately his leprosy was cleansed. And Jesus saith unto him, See thou tell no man; but go thy way, shew thyself to the priest, and offer the gift that Moses commanded, for a testimony unto them.

Mark:

And there came a leper to him, beseeching him, and kneeling down to him, and saying unto him, If thou wilt, thou canst make me clean. And Jesus, moved with compassion, put forth his hand, and touched him, and saith unto him, I will; be thou clean. And as soon as he had spoken, immediately the leprosy departed from him, and he was cleansed. And he straitly charged him, and forthwith sent him away; And saith unto him, See thou say nothing to any man: but go thy way, shew thyself to the priest, and offer for thy cleansing those things which Moses commanded, for a testimony unto them. But he went out, and began to publish it much, and to blaze abroad the matter, insomuch that Jesus could no more openly enter into the city, but was without in desert places: and they came to him from every quarter.

Luke:

And it came to pass, when he was in a certain city, behold a man full of leprosy: who seeing Jesus fell on his face, and besought him, saying, Lord, if thou wilt, thou canst make me clean. And he put forth his hand, and touched him, saying, I will: be thou clean. And immediately the leprosy departed from him. And he charged him to tell no man: but go, and shew thyself to the priest, and offer for thy cleansing, according as Moses commanded, for a testimony unto them. But so much the more went there a fame abroad of him: and great multitudes came together to hear, and to be healed by him of their infirmities.

- ❖ The miracle happened immediately.
- ❖ This man believed Jesus *could* heal him, but he did not have faith that Jesus *would* heal him.
- ❖ Even though the man didn't have the faith that takes healing on his own, he received the miracle through Jesus's faith (the one ministering).
- ❖ Jesus said, "I will." It is always God's will to heal.
- ❖ Jesus laid hands on him, as it says Jesus touched him.
- ❖ Jesus gave the command, "Be thou clean." Here the healing manifested at a simple command.
- ❖ The leper stepped out to get healed because he desired it; God did not seek him out.

Account 3: A Centurion's Sick Servant Is Healed
Matthew 8:5–13, Luke 7:1–10

Matthew:

And when Jesus was entered into Capernaum, there came unto him a centurion, beseeching him, And saying, Lord, my servant lieth at home sick of the palsy, grievously tormented. And Jesus saith unto him, I will come and heal him. The centurion answered and said, Lord, I am not worthy that thou shouldest come under my roof: but speak the word only, and my servant shall be healed. For I am a man under authority, having soldiers under me: and I say to this man, Go, and he goeth; and to another, Come, and he cometh; and to my servant, Do this, and he doeth it. When Jesus heard it, he marvelled, and said to them that followed, Verily I say unto you, I have not found so great faith, no, not in Israel. And I say unto you, That many shall come from the east and west, and shall sit down with Abraham, and Isaac, and Jacob, in the kingdom of heaven. But the children of the kingdom shall be cast out into outer darkness: there shall be weeping and gnashing of teeth. And Jesus said unto the centurion, Go thy way; and as thou hast believed, so be it done unto thee. And his servant was healed in the selfsame hour.

Luke:

Now when he had ended all his sayings in the audience of the people, he entered into Capernaum. And a certain centurion's servant, who was dear unto him, was sick, and ready to die. And when he heard of Jesus, he sent unto him the elders of the

Jews, beseeching him that he would come and heal his servant. And when they came to Jesus, they besought him instantly, saying, That he was worthy for whom he should do this: For he loveth our nation, and he hath built us a synagogue. Then Jesus went with them. And when he was now not far from the house, the centurion sent friends to him, saying unto him, Lord, trouble not thyself: for I am not worthy that thou shouldest enter under my roof: Wherefore neither thought I myself worthy to come unto thee: but say in a word, and my servant shall be healed. For I also am a man set under authority, having under me soldiers, and I say unto one, Go, and he goeth; and to another, Come, and he cometh; and to my servant, Do this, and he doeth it. When Jesus heard these things, he marvelled at him, and turned him about, and said unto the people that followed him, I say unto you, I have not found so great faith, no, not in Israel. And they that were sent, returning to the house, found the servant whole that had been sick.

- ❖ The healing manifested immediately (in the same hour).
- ❖ We looked at this account earlier in the book, but to recap, this shows us that someone can be healed based on someone else's faith. Jesus said, "As *thou* hast believed, so be it done unto thee."

- ❖ Jesus didn't have to lay his hands on the person who was healed, he spoke the word only.
- ❖ Jesus did not have to be present with the sick person.
- ❖ Jesus did not have to talk to the sick person.
- ❖ Jesus didn't say a command in this case (such as, "be thou clean"); he basically said, "As the centurion believed, so be it" (he agreed with the centurion). The centurion already spoke the faith statement when he said, "Speak the word only, and my servant shall be healed."
- ❖ The *centurion* decided the *how* in this case of healing. He had faith for his servant to be healed a certain way, and that is what he received.
- ❖ This is the only account where Jesus marveled at someone's faith. He was impressed at how confident the centurion was. This shows that God *likes* when we are bold about what we request and what we demand according to his promises.
- ❖ God did not decide if the servant would be healed, the centurion did.

Account 4: Woman with Fever Healed
Matthew 8:14–15, Mark 1:29–31, Luke 4:38–39

Matthew:

"And when Jesus was come into Peter's house, he saw his wife's mother laid, and sick of a fever. And he touched her hand, and the fever left her: and she arose, and ministered unto them."

Mark:

> And forthwith, when they were come out of the synagogue, they entered into the house of Simon and Andrew, with James and John. But Simon's wife's mother lay sick of a fever, and anon they tell him of her. And he came and took her by the hand, and lifted her up; and immediately the fever left her, and she ministered unto them.

Luke:

"And he arose out of the synagogue, and entered into Simon's house. And Simon's wife's mother was taken with a great fever; and they besought him for her. And he stood over her, and rebuked the fever; and it left her: and immediately she arose and ministered unto them."

- ❖ She was healed immediately.
- ❖ Jesus touched her, took her by the hand, and lifted her up. Him lifting her up was a faith "action."

❖ Jesus rebuked the fever. He spoke directly to the ailment. (This word "rebuked" is the same word used when he rebuked the wind and the waves.)

Account 5: Multitudes Are Healed
Matthew 8:16–17, Mark 1:32–34, Luke 4:40–41

Matthew:

When the even was come, they brought unto him many that were possessed with devils: and he cast out the spirits with his word, and healed all that were sick: That it might be fulfilled which was spoken by Esaias the prophet, saying, Himself took our infirmities, and bare our sicknesses.

Mark:

And at even, when the sun did set, they brought unto him all that were diseased, and them that were possessed with devils. And all the city was gathered together at the door. And he healed many that were sick of divers diseases, and cast out many devils; and suffered not the devils to speak, because they knew him.

Luke:

Now when the sun was setting, all they that had any sick with divers diseases brought them unto him; and he laid his hands on every one of them, and healed them. And devils also came out of many, crying out, and saying, Thou art Christ the Son of God. And he rebuking them suffered them not to speak: for they knew that he was Christ.

- ❖ Jesus healed *all* that were sick (and there were many).
- ❖ He laid hands on every one of them.
- ❖ No one in the multitude was turned away or left not healed. Surely if it were not God's will in certain circumstances, we would have seen that some did not get their healing. He healed every single one of them.
- ❖ Jesus took our infirmities and bore our sicknesses *for us* so that we could be healed.

Account 6: Paralyzed Man Brought in on Mat Healed
Matthew 9:2–8, Mark 2:1–12, Luke 5:17–25

Matthew:

And, behold, they brought to him a man sick of the palsy, lying on a bed: and Jesus seeing their faith said unto the sick of the palsy; Son, be of good cheer; thy sins be forgiven thee. And, behold, certain of the scribes said within themselves, This man blasphemeth. And Jesus knowing their thoughts said, Wherefore think ye evil in your hearts? For whether is easier, to say, Thy sins be forgiven thee; or to say, Arise, and walk? But that ye may know that the Son of man hath power on earth to forgive sins, (then saith he to the sick of the palsy,) Arise, take up thy bed, and go unto thine house. And he arose, and departed to his house. But when the multitudes saw it, they marvelled, and glorified God, which had given such power unto men.

Mark:

And again he entered into Capernaum after some days; and it was noised that he was in the house. And straightway many were gathered together, insomuch that there was no room to receive them, no, not so much as about the door: and he preached the word unto them. And they come unto him, bringing one sick of the palsy, which was borne of four. And when they could not come nigh unto him for the press, they uncovered the roof where he was: and when they had broken it up, they let down the bed wherein the sick of the palsy lay. When Jesus saw their faith, he said unto the sick of the palsy, Son, thy sins be forgiven thee. But there were certain of the scribes sitting there, and reasoning in their hearts, Why doth this man thus speak blasphemies? who can forgive sins but God only? And immediately when Jesus perceived in his spirit that they so reasoned within themselves, he said unto them, Why reason ye these things in your hearts? Whether is it easier to say to the sick of the palsy, Thy sins be forgiven thee; or to say, Arise, and take up thy bed, and walk? But that ye may know that the Son of man hath power on earth to forgive sins, (he saith to the sick of the palsy,) I say unto thee, Arise, and take up thy bed, and go thy way into thine house. And immediately he arose, took up the bed, and went forth before them all; insomuch that they were all amazed, and glorified God, saying, We never saw it on this fashion.

Luke:

And it came to pass on a certain day, as he was teaching, that there were Pharisees and doctors of the law sitting by, which were come out of every town of Galilee, and Judaea, and Jerusalem: and the power of the Lord was present to heal them. And, behold, men brought in a bed a man which was taken with a palsy: and they sought means to bring him in, and to lay him before him. And when they could not find by what way they might bring him in because of the multitude, they went upon the housetop, and let him down through the tiling with his couch into the midst before Jesus. And when he saw their faith, he said unto him, Man, thy sins are forgiven thee. And the scribes and the Pharisees began to reason, saying, Who is this which speaketh blasphemies? Who can forgive sins, but God alone? But when Jesus perceived their thoughts, he answering said unto them, What reason ye in your hearts? Whether is easier, to say, Thy sins be forgiven thee; or to say, Rise up and walk? But that ye may know that the Son of man hath power upon earth to forgive sins, (he said unto the sick of the palsy,) I say unto thee, Arise, and take up thy couch, and go into thine house. And immediately he rose up before them, and took up that whereon he lay, and departed to his own house, glorifying God.

❖ The healing was immediate.
❖ The same power to forgive sins is the same power to heal.
❖ The man was healed due to the faith of those carrying him in, not his own faith.
❖ The men did whatever it took to reach Jesus, that was faith in action. Their actions testified of their faith! It says Jesus *saw* their faith; it doesn't say he perceived it in his spirit. Faith actions are *visible* in the natural realm. What are your faith actions (works)?

Account 7 and 8: Jairus's Daughter Raised from the Dead and Woman with Issue of Blood Healed
Matthew 9:18–26, Mark 5:21–43, Luke 8:40–55

These are two different occurrences, but they overlap one another.

Matthew:

> While he spake these things unto them, behold, there came a certain ruler, and worshipped him, saying, My daughter is even now dead: but come and lay thy hand upon her, and she shall live. And Jesus arose, and followed him, and so did his disciples. And, behold, a woman, which was diseased with an issue of blood twelve years, came behind him, and touched the hem of his garment: For she said within herself, If I may but touch his garment, I shall be whole. But Jesus turned him about, and when he saw her, he said, Daughter, be of good comfort; thy faith hath made thee whole. And the woman was made whole from that hour. And when Jesus came into the ruler's house, and saw the minstrels and the people making a noise, He said unto them, Give place: for the maid is not dead, but sleepeth. And they laughed him to scorn. But when the people were put forth, he went in, and took her by the hand, and the maid arose. And the fame hereof went abroad into all that land.

Mark:

And when Jesus was passed over again by ship unto the other side, much people gathered unto him: and he was nigh unto the sea. And, behold, there cometh one of the rulers of the synagogue, Jairus by name; and when he saw him, he fell at his feet, And besought him greatly, saying, My little daughter lieth at the point of death: I pray thee, come and lay thy hands on her, that she may be healed; and she shall live. And Jesus went with him; and much people followed him, and thronged him. And a certain woman, which had an issue of blood twelve years, And had suffered many things of many physicians, and had spent all that she had, and was nothing bettered, but rather grew worse, When she had heard of Jesus, came in the press behind, and touched his garment. For she said, If I may touch but his clothes, I shall be whole. And straightway the fountain of her blood was dried up; and she felt in her body that she was healed of that plague. And Jesus, immediately knowing in himself that virtue had gone out of him, turned him about in the press, and said, Who touched my clothes? And his disciples said unto him, Thou seest the multitude thronging thee, and sayest thou, Who touched me? And he looked round about to see her that had done this thing. But the woman fearing and trembling, knowing what was done in her, came and fell down before him, and told him all the truth. And he said unto her, Daughter, thy faith hath made thee whole; go in peace, and be whole of thy plague. While he yet spake, there came from the ruler of the synagogue's house certain which said, Thy daughter is dead: why troublest thou the Master any further? As soon as Jesus heard the word that was spoken, he saith unto the ruler of the synagogue, Be not afraid, only believe. And he suffered no man to follow him, save Peter, and James, and John the brother of James. And he cometh to the house of the ruler of the synagogue, and seeth the tumult, and them that wept and wailed greatly. And when he was come in, he saith unto them, Why make ye this ado, and weep? the damsel is not dead, but sleepeth. And they laughed him to scorn. But when he had put them all out, he taketh the father and the mother of the damsel, and them that were with him, and entereth in where the damsel was lying. And he took the damsel by the hand, and said unto her, Talitha cumi; which is, being interpreted, Damsel, I say unto thee, arise. And straightway the damsel arose, and walked; for she was of the age of twelve years. And they were astonished with a great astonishment. And he charged them straitly that no man should know it; and commanded that something should be given her to eat.

Luke:

And it came to pass, that, when Jesus was returned, the people gladly received him: for they were all waiting for him. And, behold, there came a man named Jairus, and he was a ruler of the synagogue: and he fell down at Jesus' feet, and besought him that he would come into his house: For he had one only daughter, about twelve years of age, and she lay a dying. But as he went the people thronged him. And a woman having an issue of blood twelve years, which had spent all her living upon physicians, neither could be healed of any, Came behind him, and touched the border of his garment: and immediately her issue of blood stanched. And Jesus said, Who touched me? When all denied, Peter and they that were with him said, Master, the multitude throng thee and press thee, and sayest thou, Who touched me? And Jesus said, Somebody hath touched me: for I perceive that virtue is gone out of me. And when the woman saw that she was not hid, she came trembling, and falling down before him, she declared unto him before all the people for what cause she had touched him, and how she was healed immediately. And he said unto her, Daughter, be of good comfort: thy faith hath made thee whole; go in peace. While he yet spake, there cometh one from the ruler of the synagogue's house, saying to him, Thy daughter is dead; trouble not the Master. But when Jesus heard it, he answered him, saying, Fear not: believe only, and she shall be made whole. And when he came into the house, he suffered no man to go in, save Peter, and James, and John, and the father and the mother of the maiden. And all wept, and bewailed her: but he said, Weep not; she is not dead, but sleepeth. And they laughed him to scorn, knowing that she was dead. And he put them all out, and took her by the hand, and called, saying, Maid, arise. And her spirit came again, and she arose straightway: and he commanded to give her meat.

Facts surrounding Jairus's miracle:

❖ Healing is available no matter how advanced the situation: his daughter was at the point of death when he sought Jesus out.

❖ Jairus made a faith statement, "Come and lay thy hands on her, that she may be healed; and she shall live."

❖ She was not healed (raised from the dead) on her own faith.

- Jesus went with Jairus to do as he asked at Jairus's request. Very simply, we put the demand on healing, we aren't waiting for God to grant it.

- The answer (Jesus) was already on its way for the manifestation. During that time period between the miracle being released and it manifesting, the situation in the natural appeared worse (in this case the daughter died, so it got as bad as it could get), and yet none of that had any bearing on the manifestation. In our own circumstances, we believe the healing is already granted when we pray, and even if circumstances seem worse, we expect that it will still manifest.

- When Jairus got the bad report that his daughter was now dead, Jesus immediately responded to it and told Jairus to stop the fear and only believe. We also must stop any negative report or circumstance from taking root in our spirit that is contrary to God's word, *immediately*. The longer you meditate on it and entertain it, the deeper the roots become, and it is more work to get it uprooted from your heart. This is not just a doctor's report, this is daily if you feel a pain and then you allow yourself to meditate on how bad it is and get into negative thinking about that all day before you cast it down and put your eyes back on Jesus and your healing.

❖ Also see here that Jesus didn't say, "Now it's too late. I was going to come heal her, but now she is dead, and there is nothing I can do." It doesn't matter how impossible it looks or how bad the circumstances get, God's will is to heal and bring life, and his word is certain and always comes to pass. If the power that lives in us raises people from the dead, we shouldn't question whether it can heal!

❖ After the woman who had interrupted their journey had been healed and the report of the daughter dying had occurred, Jesus was then selective on who could go any further on the journey with them for the miracle. This shows us that in certain circumstances, it will be harder to receive the miracle if you aren't careful about who you let around you and their influence.

❖ When Jesus saw the evidence of the daughter being dead, which was the great sorrow and weeping of the people at Jairus's house, he asked why they were so sorrowful: she wasn't dead but asleep. I believe this is two powerful teaching points. One, Jesus weeded out who had faith and who would have the type of unbelief that blocked miracles (it says they laughed him to scorn, so that was the same type of unbelief that blocked his power to perform miracles in his own hometown.) The other side of that statement is that he was counteracting what the circumstances were trying to sow into him. He immediately challenged the circumstance that said she was dead and spoke his faith statement out loud.

❖ Then Jesus put everyone out except the people that came with him and the parents. This is important and clearly it was necessary. If you want to see miracles, keep those who think and behave the way those people did away from you! If Jesus had to do it, you do too.

❖ Jesus didn't have any struggle, he just commanded her to arise, and her spirit came back into her, and she arose.

Facts surrounding the woman's miracle:

❖ The woman was healed immediately.

❖ The woman was healed in the way that she believed for. This tells us that if we can have faith for something, we can receive it in that way.

❖ The woman made her own faith statement, as the text states, "For she said within herself, If I may but touch his garment, I shall be whole."

❖ Notice it says, "When she heard of Jesus." This is imperative, as she was not able to make the faith statement above and then act on it without hearing about Jesus first. Faith comes by hearing, and we need to be hearing constantly what God's word says concerning healing. If we are ministering to someone else, they need to hear about the truth of God's word regarding healing as well for faith to come.

❖ This woman risked everything to get to Jesus. She was not to be out in public with the condition she had or touching anyone, because she was unclean. She was so convinced that she would be healed that she pressed through a crowd of people to get to Jesus.

❖ Jesus did not grant this woman's healing, nor did she ask Jesus to heal her. She *took* her healing at her desire and on her faith. You can do the same.

We are not waiting on permission from God for anything related to healing; it was already granted.

❖ This woman had tried everything the doctors could offer, spent all that she had, and was not better, but was instead worse, and yet the power of God healed her. This is an account of someone with an incurable disease (like many of the other accounts in the word) and should convince you that God's word works even in those situations without restriction!

❖ Jesus perceived the virtue (power) go out of him.

❖ Jesus made a point to tell her that it was her faith that made her whole, and this teaches us that it is one of the methods by which healing miracles occur so we can get the same result.

Account 9: Two Blind Men Healed
Matthew 9:27–31

And when Jesus departed thence, two blind men followed him, crying, and saying, Thou son of David, have mercy on us. And when he was come into the house, the blind men came to him: and Jesus saith unto them, Believe ye that I am able to do this? They said unto him, Yea, Lord. Then touched he their eyes, saying, According to your faith be it unto you. And their eyes were opened; and Jesus straitly charged them, saying, See that no man know it. But they, when they were departed, spread abroad his fame in all that country.

- ❖ When they cried, "Thou son of David," they were recognizing and making a faith statement of their belief in who Jesus was.
- ❖ Jesus asked if they believed he was able to perform the miracle, and they said with their mouth yes, which was also positioning them in faith to receive.
- ❖ Jesus said, "According to your faith be it unto you," which is Jesus showing us how the miracle was received.
- ❖ The men were healed immediately.
- ❖ The men sought Jesus out for their healing because they desired it. It was not up to God; it was at their desire and by their faith.

Account 10: A Dumb (Mute) Man Healed
Matthew 9:32–33

"As they went out, behold, they brought to him a dumb man possessed with a devil. And when the devil was cast out, the dumb spake: and the multitudes marvelled, saying, It was never so seen in Israel."

- ❖ This man was healed immediately.
- ❖ It notes that after the devil was cast out he spoke, telling us that a demon was the root of the problem and was responsible for the physical issue.
- ❖ If this was the case then, there will be cases now where a physical issue will only be resolved when the demon is cast out.

Account 11: Every Sickness and Disease Healed
Matthew 9:35

"And Jesus went about all the cities and villages, teaching in their synagogues, and preaching the gospel of the kingdom, and healing every sickness and every disease among the people."

- ❖ This attests to the fact that Jesus's ministry included preaching the gospel and performing miracles as a whole, and ours should as well.
- ❖ It says he healed *every* sickness and *every* disease among the people. There was no issue that could not be healed, and there were no people who did not get healed!

Account 12: A Man with a Withered Hand Healed
Matthew 12:9–13, Mark 3:1–5, Luke 6:6–10

Matthew:

And when he was departed thence, he went into their synagogue: And, behold, there was a man which had his hand withered. And they asked him, saying, Is it lawful to heal on the sabbath days? that they might accuse him. And he said unto them, What man shall there be among you, that shall have one sheep, and if it fall into a pit on the sabbath day, will he not lay hold on it, and lift it out? How much then is a man better than a sheep? Wherefore it is lawful to do well on the sabbath days. Then saith he to the man, Stretch forth thine hand. And he stretched it forth; and it was restored whole, like as the other.

Mark:

And he entered again into the synagogue; and there was a man there which had a withered hand. And they watched him, whether he would heal him on the sabbath day; that they might accuse him. And he saith unto the man which had the withered hand, Stand forth. And he saith unto them, Is it lawful to do good on the sabbath days, or to do evil? to save life, or to kill? But they held their peace. And when he had looked round about on them with anger, being grieved for the hardness of their hearts, he saith unto the man, Stretch forth thine hand. And he stretched it out: and his hand was restored whole as the other.

Luke:

And it came to pass also on another sabbath, that he entered into the synagogue and taught: and there was a man whose right hand was withered. And the scribes and Pharisees watched him, whether he would heal on the sabbath day; that they might find an accusation against him. But he knew their thoughts, and said to the man which had the withered hand, Rise up, and stand forth in the midst. And he arose and stood forth. Then said Jesus unto them, I will ask you one thing; Is it lawful on the sabbath days to do good, or to do evil? to save life, or to destroy it? And looking round about upon them all, he said unto the man, Stretch forth thy hand. And he did so: and his hand was restored whole as the other.

❖ This sums up that there really is no time when it is against God's laws for healing to be available.
❖ The man did not seek the healing on his own, Jesus saw him and told him to stand forth out in the midst of the people.

- This is an account where God chose at his own desire to heal the man for a specific purpose, showing us that this is one of the methods in which healing occurs.

- Jesus commanded the man to stretch forth his hand, showing us again that healing is simple and does not require long, drawn-out prayers. (Longer prayers are not wrong, as stated elsewhere in this book, as they help us to really get our heart focused on God's word and deal with unbelief as we release words of faith.)

- Jesus did not command the man's hand to be whole, he just said in faith to stretch it forth, as the man could not do that before, and to stretch it forth would mean that it was whole. There are different ways to speak a healing command.

- The man was not healed on his own faith; however, he was obedient in what Jesus told him to do.

- The man was healed immediately.

Account 13: Multitude Healed
Matthew 12:15, Mark 3:7–10, Luke 6:17–19

Matthew:

"But when Jesus knew it, he withdrew himself from thence: and great multitudes followed him, and he healed them all."

Mark:

But Jesus withdrew himself with his disciples to the sea: and a great multitude from Galilee followed him, and from Judaea, And from Jerusalem, and from Idumaea, and from beyond Jordan; and they about Tyre and Sidon, a great multitude, when they had heard what great things he did, came unto him. And he spake to his disciples, that a small ship should wait on him because of the multitude, lest they should throng him. For he had healed many; insomuch that they pressed upon him for to touch him, as many as had plagues.

Luke:

And he came down with them, and stood in the plain, and the company of his disciples, and a great multitude of people out of all Judaea and Jerusalem, and from the sea coast of Tyre and Sidon, which came to hear him, and to be healed of their diseases; And they that were vexed with unclean spirits: and they were healed. And the whole multitude sought to touch him: for there went virtue out of him, and healed them all.

- ❖ Jesus healed them all. From diseases to those vexed with unclean spirits.
- ❖ No one was left sick; no situation was too difficult for God to heal.
- ❖ If they were all healed, then this shows that there is never a time when it is not God's will to heal. There was a great multitude, so we can confidently estimate that there would have been all types of people (from young to old) ranging in different places spiritually. You are not a "worse" Christian than every one of those people, you are not the exception that God needs to teach you something. This shows us that those concepts are unscriptural. He healed them *all*.

Account 14: A Blind, Dumb, and Possessed Man Healed
Matthew 12:22

Matthew:

"Then was brought unto him one possessed with a devil, blind, and dumb: and he healed him, insomuch that the blind and dumb both spake and saw."

- ❖ The man was healed immediately.
- ❖ The sickness was due to a demon, and the demon had to be cast out for the physical symptoms to change.

Account 15: A Multitude Healed
Matthew 14:14

"And Jesus went forth, and saw a great multitude, and was moved with compassion toward them, and he healed their sick."

- ❖ This shows the heart of God: he has great compassion for us in his love for us. He wants us well; he does not want us suffering!
- ❖ Jesus simply healed their sick. We see here again that no one was untouched by him if they desired healing.

Account 16: A Multitude Healed
Matthew 14:35–36

"And when the men of that place had knowledge of him, they sent out into all that country round about, and brought unto him all that were diseased; And besought him that they might only touch the hem of his garment: and as many as touched were made perfectly whole."

- ❖ The people had faith to be healed in a certain manner, and they received it when they acted in faith by doing what they believed for. They didn't have to touch his garment to be healed; we have seen many accounts where Jesus healed in certain ways. However, this is what *they* had faith for, and thus they received it in that manner. Jesus didn't tell them to touch his garment, that is what they said. We have a say *how* we are healed.

❖ Every single person who acted in faith received healing. Again, God didn't say to anyone it wasn't their time, that they still had more to learn before they could be healed, that it wasn't his will to heal them, or that they still needed to be punished for something a little longer before they could be healed. That is not scriptural, and in none of the accounts did Jesus say this!

❖ The people got their healing because they desired it, they didn't wait for God to grant it.

Account 17: A Multitude Healed
Matthew 15:30–31

And great multitudes came unto him, having with them those that were lame, blind, dumb, maimed, and many others, and cast them down at Jesus' feet; and he healed them: Insomuch that the multitude wondered, when they saw the dumb to speak, the maimed to be whole, the lame to walk, and the blind to see: and they glorified the God of Israel.

- ❖ No one was turned away: everyone (with various diseases) was healed. Every single one.
- ❖ There was no issue too difficult to receive healing right then on the spot.

Account 18: An Epileptic Boy Healed
Matthew 17:14–21, Mark 9:14–29, Luke 9:37–42

Matthew:

And when they were come to the multitude, there came to him a certain man, kneeling down to him, and saying, Lord, have mercy on my son: for he is lunatick, and sore vexed: for ofttimes he falleth into the fire, and oft into the water. And I brought him to thy disciples, and they could not cure him. Then Jesus answered and said, O faithless and perverse generation, how long shall I be with you? how long shall I suffer you? bring him hither to me. And Jesus rebuked the devil; and he departed out of him: and the child was cured from that very hour. Then came the disciples to Jesus apart, and said, Why could not we cast him out? And Jesus said unto them, Because of your unbelief: for verily I say unto you, If ye have faith as a grain of mustard seed, ye shall say unto this mountain, Remove hence to yonder place; and it shall remove; and nothing shall be impossible unto you. Howbeit this kind goeth not out but by prayer and fasting.

Mark:

And when he came to his disciples, he saw a great multitude about them, and the scribes questioning with them. And straightway all the people, when they beheld him, were greatly amazed, and running to him saluted him. And he asked the scribes, What question ye with them? And one of the multitude answered and said, Master, I have brought unto thee my son, which hath a dumb spirit; And wheresoever he taketh him, he teareth him: and he foameth, and gnasheth with his teeth, and pineth away: and I spake to thy disciples that they should cast him out; and they could not. He answereth him, and saith, O faithless generation, how long shall I be with you? how long shall I suffer you? bring him unto me. And they brought him unto him: and when he saw him, straightway the spirit tare him; and he fell on the ground, and wallowed foaming. And he asked his father, How long is it ago since this came unto him? And he said, Of a child. And ofttimes it hath cast him into the fire, and into the waters, to destroy him: but if thou canst do any thing, have compassion on us, and help us. Jesus said unto him, If thou canst believe, all things are possible to him that believeth. And straightway the father of the child cried out, and said with tears, Lord, I believe; help thou mine unbelief. When Jesus saw that the people came running together, he rebuked the foul spirit, saying unto him, Thou dumb and deaf spirit, I charge thee, come out of him, and enter no more into him. And the spirit cried, and rent him sore, and came out of him: and he was as one dead; insomuch that many said, He is dead. But Jesus took him by the hand, and lifted him up; and he arose. And when he was come into the house, his disciples asked him privately, Why could not we cast him out? And he said unto them, This kind can come forth by nothing, but by prayer and fasting.

Luke:

And it came to pass, that on the next day, when they were come down from the hill, much people met him. And, behold, a man of the company cried out, saying, Master, I beseech thee, look upon my son: for he is mine only child. And, lo, a spirit taketh him, and he suddenly crieth out; and it teareth him that he foameth again, and bruising him hardly departeth from him. And I besought thy disciples to cast him out; and they could not. And Jesus answering said, O

217

faithless and perverse generation, how long shall I be with you, and suffer you? Bring thy son hither. And as he was yet a coming, the devil threw him down, and tare him. And Jesus rebuked the unclean spirit, and healed the child, and delivered him again to his father.

- ❖ The boy was healed immediately.

- ❖ The boy was not healed on his own faith.

- ❖ The root cause of the illness was a demon, and Jesus had to cast it out.

- ❖ The disciples had already experienced miracles and were confused as to why they could not do it in this case.
- ❖ Jesus said the disciples could not do the miracle because of their unbelief.

- ❖ Jesus was extremely upset that the disciples were not able to heal the boy. This shows us he fully expects his command for us to go heal the sick and cast out devils to be something we follow through with, and he fully expects us to *be able* to do it.

❖ Jesus asked the father how long the boy had dealt with the issue, and the father said since he was a child. Jesus never asked anything unless there was a reason for it. I believe this shows us that the length of time we have been dealing with a situation has an impact on our coming out of it. The longer we have been looking at a sickness in our lives, the bigger of a stronghold it has in our hearts. It even becomes part of our identity, as we think about life choices and daily experiences as a whole with that sickness in mind.

❖ Jesus told the disciples that "this kind" does not go out but by prayer and fasting. He was not talking about a more powerful demon! The topic and the reason they couldn't cast the demon out was due to their unbelief. If it was because the demon was more powerful, he would have said that instead. No demon has enough power to withstand the name of Jesus. This shows us that fasting is a requirement for some miracles to manifest because through prayer and fasting we can deal with more deep-seated unbelief that is more difficult to push out. I think it is easier to combat unbelief in our hearts in certain circumstances than it is in others. Sometimes that may be because a sickness has been there so many years that it takes those times in fasting with prayer to break through to see yourself healed. Other times it may be the severity of the miracle needed (for example, someone at home on hospice with days left to live) that our faith needs the combination of fasting with prayer.

❖ Here Jesus clearly made it a point to tell the disciples it only takes faith as the grain of a mustard seed; it was their unbelief that was the problem. They had faith. This is a prime example of what we've seen in relation to the progression of a miracle diagram earlier in this book. It shows that faith can be present as needed, but a block (in this case unbelief) stops the manifestation.

Account 19: A Multitude Healed
Matthew 19:1–2

"And it came to pass, that when Jesus had finished these sayings, he departed from Galilee, and came into the coasts of Judaea beyond Jordan; And great multitudes followed him; and he healed them there."

❖ He healed them! Jesus was constantly healing all throughout his ministry, including large numbers of people. We can never question the fact that it is God's will to heal every single time.

Account 20: Two Blind Men Healed
Matthew 20:30–34, Mark 10:46–52, Luke 18:35–43

Matthew:

> And, behold, two blind men sitting by the way side, when they heard that Jesus passed by, cried out, saying, Have mercy on us, O Lord, thou Son of David. And the multitude rebuked them, because they should hold their peace: but they cried the more, saying, Have mercy on us, O Lord, thou Son of David. And Jesus stood still, and called them, and said, What will ye that I shall do unto you? They say unto him, Lord, that our eyes may be opened. So Jesus had compassion on them, and touched their eyes: and immediately their eyes received sight, and they followed him.

Mark:

> And they came to Jericho: and as he went out of Jericho with his disciples and a great number of people, blind Bartimaeus, the son of Timaeus, sat by the highway side begging. And when he heard that it was Jesus of Nazareth, he began to cry out, and say, Jesus, thou Son of David, have mercy on me. And many charged him that he should hold his peace: but

he cried the more a great deal, Thou Son of David, have mercy on me. And Jesus stood still, and commanded him to be called. And they call the blind man, saying unto him, Be of good comfort, rise; he calleth thee. And he, casting away his garment, rose, and came to Jesus. And Jesus answered and said unto him, What wilt thou that I should do unto thee? The blind man said unto him, Lord, that I might receive my sight. And Jesus said unto him, Go thy way; thy faith hath made thee whole. And immediately he received his sight, and followed Jesus in the way.

Luke:

And it came to pass, that as he was come nigh unto Jericho, a certain blind man sat by the way side begging: And hearing the multitude pass by, he asked what it meant. And they told him, that Jesus of Nazareth passeth by. And he cried, saying, Jesus, thou Son of David, have mercy on me. And they which went before rebuked him, that he should hold his peace: but he cried so much the more, Thou Son of David, have mercy on me. And Jesus stood, and commanded him to be brought unto him: and when he was come near, he asked him, Saying, What wilt thou that I shall do unto thee? And he said, Lord, that I may receive my sight. And Jesus said unto him,

Receive thy sight: thy faith hath saved thee. And immediately he received his sight, and followed him, glorifying God: and all the people, when they saw it, gave praise unto God.

❖ The men were healed immediately.

❖ Two of the accounts tell us who one of the men was specifically, the other account lets us know there was another blind man who received his sight as well.

❖ They called Jesus, "Thou Son of David," making a faith statement recognizing him for who he was.

❖ When the crowd told them to be quiet, they cried even louder. They refused every opposing voice to their miracle and just pushed harder in the face of opposition.

❖ It says Jesus stood still. Now *that* should get our attention in a big way. The cries of faith and persistence, with a refusal to back off their expectation of healing, caused Jesus to stop in his tracks. Our faith and demand on the healing covenant always causes healing to come.

❖ Not only did it cause Jesus to stand still, but then he asked what it was they desired that he could do for them!! And we think God doesn't want to heal us?! We go full force in prayer in faith, and this is the response we get from our God, period.

- Then they made the request for sight, and they got it. It was that simple for them to receive their healing.
- Here we see that Jesus just touched their eyes and told them to receive their sight. He also made the point to say that their faith had made them whole.

Account 21: A Deaf and Dumb (Mute) Man Healed
Mark 7:32–37

And they bring unto him one that was deaf, and had an impediment in his speech; and they beseech him to put his hand upon him. And he took him aside from the multitude, and put his fingers into his ears, and he spit, and touched his tongue; And looking up to heaven, he sighed, and saith unto him, Ephphatha, that is, Be opened. And straightway his ears were opened, and the string of his tongue was loosed, and he spake plain. And he charged them that they should tell no man: but the more he charged them, so much the more a great deal they published it; And were beyond measure astonished, saying, He hath done all things well: he maketh both the deaf to hear, and the dumb to speak.

- Jesus took this man away from the crowd.

❖ Jesus did something uncommon in that he put his fingers in his ears and spit and touched his tongue.

❖ The command he gave here was, "Be opened." In this case he spoke directly to the parts of the body that were affected and commanded them to be opened. This would indicate that his faith command was to loose them from what was binding them from functioning properly.

❖ The man was healed immediately.

Account 22: A Blind Man Healed
Mark 8:22–26

And he cometh to Bethsaida; and they bring a blind man unto him, and besought him to touch him. And he took the blind man by the hand, and led him out of the town; and when he had spit on his eyes, and put his hands upon him, he asked him if he saw ought. And he looked up, and said, I see men as trees, walking. After that he put his hands again upon his eyes, and made him look up: and he was restored, and saw every man clearly. And he sent him away to his house, saying, Neither go into the town, nor tell it to any in the town.

❖ Jesus took this man away from the crowd.

❖ Jesus did something uncommon by spitting on his eyes and then putting his hands on him.
❖ Jesus asked if he saw as he should, thus he tested the healing.
❖ In this case, Jesus had to put his hands on the man a second time, and his full sight was restored. This tells us that when we don't see the manifestation immediately, we don't give up.

Account 23: A Man's Ear That Was Cut off Healed
Luke 22:50–51

"And one of them smote the servant of the high priest, and cut off his right ear. And Jesus answered and said, Suffer ye thus far. And he touched his ear, and healed him."

❖ This was when the men came to take Jesus captive, and his disciple cut off one of the men's ears. If it was God's will to heal and not harm this man, then it is definitely God's will to heal you!
❖ Jesus healed this man's ear by simply touching it.

Account 24: A Widow's Son Raised from the Dead
Luke 7:12–17

Now when he came nigh to the gate of the city, behold, there was a dead man carried out, the only son of his mother, and she was a widow: and much people of the city was with her. And when the Lord saw her, he had compassion on her, and said unto her, Weep not. And he came and touched the bier: and they that bare him stood still. And he said, Young man, I say unto thee, Arise. And he that was dead sat up, and began to speak. And he delivered him to his mother. And there came a fear on all: and they glorified God, saying, That a great prophet is risen up among us; and, That God hath visited his people. And this rumour of him went forth throughout all Judaea, and throughout all the region round about.

- ❖ God chose to perform this miracle (the mother did not seek Jesus out for it). He was moved with compassion when he saw her and just did it.
- ❖ He first comforted her by telling her not to weep.
- ❖ He touched the coffin and raised him from the dead by simply telling the young man to arise.
- ❖ The miracle manifested immediately.
- ❖ It is easy for God to raise people from the dead; we must have faith that we will see these things if we want to see them happen. If you don't begin with saying in your heart that you will operate in God's power to raise people from the dead, you

never will. You can't do anything you don't have faith for. Remember, Jesus told us to raise the dead. He did it, and he told us to go out and do it. Same thing for healing.

Account 25: A Dumb (Mute) Man Healed
Luke 11:14

"And he was casting out a devil, and it was dumb. And it came to pass, when the devil was gone out, the dumb spake; and the people wondered."

- ❖ The man was healed immediately.
- ❖ It says the devil was dumb (mute). This perhaps indicates that certain demonic spirits have identities and are associated with different illnesses.
- ❖ Casting the devil out caused the man to speak, thus the physical symptoms were caused directly by the demon.

Account 26: A Woman with a Spirit of Infirmity Healed
Luke 13:10–17

And he was teaching in one of the synagogues on the sabbath. And, behold, there was a woman which had a spirit of infirmity eighteen years, and was bowed together, and could in no wise lift up herself. And when Jesus saw her, he called her to him, and said unto her, Woman, thou art loosed from thine infirmity. And he laid his hands on her: and immediately she was made straight, and glorified God. And the ruler of the synagogue answered with indignation, because that Jesus had healed on the sabbath day, and said unto the people, There are six days in which men ought to work: in them therefore come and be healed, and not on the sabbath day. The Lord then answered him, and said, Thou hypocrite, doth not each one of you on the sabbath loose his ox or his ass from the stall, and lead him away to watering? And ought not this woman, being a daughter of Abraham, whom Satan hath bound, lo, these eighteen years, be loosed from this bond on the sabbath day? And when he had said these things, all his adversaries were ashamed: and all the people rejoiced for all the glorious things that were done by him.

❖ The woman was healed immediately.

❖ The woman's physical symptoms were caused by a demon.

❖ It calls the demon a spirit of infirmity, again indicating that there are different types of demons, or perhaps a better way to say it is that different demons work in people in different ways.

❖ Jesus cast the devil out by speaking directly to the woman, decreeing she was loosed from her infirmity (released from bondage). Then he laid his hands on her, and immediately her back was healed, and she could stand straight.

❖ This shows that Christians (not just those who aren't saved) can be affected by demonic spirits causing sickness, as it states she was a daughter of Abraham. Jesus had to cast the devil out of her for her to be free, so that means that this may still be the root issue that needs to be dealt with, even if someone is a Christian.

❖ The ruler of the synagogue there questioned Jesus's actions, stating it wasn't right to heal being that it was the Sabbath day. And yet Jesus's response was the opposite. He essentially said, "Shouldn't she be healed even more so given that she is a daughter of Abraham (an heir to the covenant promise of healing) and has been bound by Satan all these years?" This shows us God's intent to heal, how important we are to him as his children, and what our rights are as his children.

Account 27: Ten Lepers Healed
Luke 17:12–19

And as he entered into a certain village, there met him ten men that were lepers, which stood afar off: And they lifted up their voices, and said, Jesus, Master, have mercy on us. And when he saw them, he said unto them, Go shew yourselves unto the priests. And it came to pass, that, as they went, they were cleansed. And one of them, when he saw that he was healed, turned back, and with a loud voice glorified God, And fell down on his face at his feet, giving him thanks: and he was a Samaritan. And Jesus answering said, Were there not ten cleansed? but where are the nine? There are not found that returned to give glory to God, save this stranger. And he said unto him, Arise, go thy way: thy faith hath made thee whole.

❖ The lepers vocalized their faith when they cried out to Jesus.
❖ The lepers were healed as they went. When they obeyed what Jesus told them to do, that was an act of faith. Our "faith actions" (or "faith works")

are vital, as we have already discussed in this book.

❖ Jesus didn't have to lay hands on them, he didn't even say to them, "Be healed." He just told them to go show themselves to the priest. (Which was what you would do if you were healed.) This is similar to making an appointment with your doctor to get updated results about your condition, anticipating that you will receive the news of your healing that you are expecting by faith!

❖ When the one leper came back to give thanks to God, Jesus was pointing out how ungrateful the others were, but he also used this event to relay how the man received his healing when he said, "Thy faith hath made thee whole."

Account 28: A Nobleman's Son Healed
John 4:46–53

So Jesus came again into Cana of Galilee, where he made the water wine. And there was a certain nobleman, whose son was sick at Capernaum. When he heard that Jesus was come out of Judaea into Galilee, he went unto him, and besought him that he would come down, and heal his son: for he was at the point of death. Then said Jesus unto him, Except ye see signs and wonders, ye will not believe. The nobleman saith unto him, Sir, come down ere my child die. Jesus saith unto him, Go thy way; thy son liveth. And the man believed the word that Jesus had spoken unto him, and he went his way. And as he was now going down, his servants met him, and told him, saying, Thy son liveth. Then enquired he of them the hour when he began to amend. And they said unto him, Yesterday at the seventh hour the fever left him. So the father knew that it was at the same hour, in the which Jesus said unto him, Thy son liveth: and himself believed, and his whole house.

- ❖ The boy was healed immediately.
- ❖ Jesus pointed out that this man would not believe except he "see signs and wonders," and at the end of the account, it tells us that was when the man believed (and his whole house), which was when he got news that his son was cured and realized it was at the same time (hour) that Jesus had told him his son lived.
- ❖ Jesus spoke the healing here; he didn't go with the man, nor did he lay hands on the boy.
- ❖ I believe this was a different situation than some of the others. When the man asked Jesus to come and heal his son or he would die, Jesus replied that the man would not believe without signs and wonders. The man then *again* asked Jesus to

come, otherwise his son would die. Jesus went with people in every other account where we see that they asked him to. Here he did not, but instead replied that the man wouldn't believe unless he saw signs and wonders. Then, when the man asked again, he said to the man, "Go thy way; thy son liveth." By telling the man simply that his son lived and to go, Jesus released the faith and healing power for his son's miracle, but he commanded the man to go on his own here because he was dealing with the unbelief the man had as a necessity. He was going beyond just healing his son and was dealing with this man's belief and salvation. It was the man's choice in that moment to believe just on what Jesus had said and obey him, which was his faith action.

Account 29: An Impotent Man Healed
John 5:1–15

After this there was a feast of the Jews; and Jesus went up to Jerusalem. Now there is at Jerusalem by the sheep market a pool, which is called in the Hebrew tongue Bethesda, having five porches. In these lay a great multitude of impotent folk, of blind, halt, withered, waiting for the moving of the water. For an angel went down at a certain season into the pool, and troubled the water: whosoever then first after the troubling of the water stepped in was made whole of whatsoever disease he had. And a certain man was there, which had an infirmity thirty and eight years. When Jesus saw him lie, and knew that he had been now a long time in that case, he saith unto him, Wilt thou be made whole? The impotent man answered him, Sir, I have no man, when the water is troubled, to put me into the pool: but while I am coming, another steppeth down before me. Jesus saith unto him, Rise, take up thy bed, and walk. And immediately the man was made whole, and took up his bed, and walked: and on the same day was the sabbath. The Jews therefore said unto him that was cured, It is the sabbath day: it is not lawful for thee to carry thy bed. He answered them, He that made me whole, the same said unto me, Take up thy bed, and walk. Then asked they him, What man is that which said unto thee, Take up thy bed, and walk? And he that was healed wist not who it was: for Jesus had conveyed himself away, a multitude being in that place. Afterward Jesus findeth him in the temple, and said unto him, Behold, thou art made whole: sin no more, lest a worse thing come unto thee. The man departed, and told the Jews that it was Jesus, which had made him whole.

- ❖ The man was healed immediately.

- ❖ This is another example of God choosing to heal at his own discretion for his purpose; neither this man (nor anyone else) sought out Jesus for this miracle.

- ❖ Jesus asked the man if he *would* be made whole. He was directing the man's attention to the fact that he could receive healing and and was asking him to ignore all the other reasons why he had not.

- ❖ Here Jesus told him to do something he couldn't do before when he released his faith for the miracle, and healing manifested. (We've seen in some cases that he spoke to someone's ears/tongue and said, "Be opened." In other cases, he just agreed with others' faith statements by saying, "According to your faith, be it unto you.")

- ❖ This is another account of Jesus healing on the Sabbath, completely rattling the people's religious false doctrines and showing God's will to heal everyone, all the time.

- ❖ When Jesus found the man again later in the temple, he told him to sin no more or something worse would come upon him. This is especially important because it tells us that we open doors for sickness to legally come upon us with blatant sin and disobedience. We need to be careful not

236

to get into condemnation here because that will hurt our faith, and it is not of God. However, we do need to be aware that this is a reality when it comes to the laws of healing, or Jesus would not have made a point to go find this man on purpose to be sure to tell him this.

Account 30: A Blind Man Healed
John 9:1–7

And as Jesus passed by, he saw a man which was blind from his birth. And his disciples asked him, saying, Master, who did sin, this man, or his parents, that he was born blind? Jesus answered, Neither hath this man sinned, nor his parents: but that the works of God should be made manifest in him. I must work the works of him that sent me, while it is day: the night cometh, when no man can work. As long as I am in the world, I am the light of the world. When he had thus spoken, he spat on the ground, and made clay of the spittle, and he anointed the eyes of the blind man with the clay, And said unto him, Go, wash in the pool of Siloam, (which is by interpretation, Sent.) He went his way therefore, and washed, and came seeing.

❖ This tells us that not all sickness is a result of sin.

- ❖ It does not appear that this man sought Jesus out to be healed, and thus this was another instance where God stepped in to do a miracle at his own desire for his purpose.
- ❖ Jesus did something uncommon here: he spat in the clay and rubbed the clay on the man's eyes.
- ❖ Jesus told the man to go wash in the pool of Siloam. The man, being obedient to Jesus's instruction, took a faith action.
- ❖ The man was healed immediately when he acted on what Jesus told him to do.

Account 31: Lazarus Is Raised from the Dead
John 11:1–45

Now a certain man was sick, named Lazarus, of Bethany, the town of Mary and her sister Martha (It was that Mary which anointed the Lord with ointment, and wiped his feet with her hair, whose brother Lazarus was sick.) Therefore his sisters sent unto him, saying, Lord, behold, he whom thou lovest is sick. When Jesus heard that, he said, This sickness is not unto death, but for the glory of God, that the Son of God might be glorified thereby. Now Jesus loved Martha, and her sister, and Lazarus. When he had heard therefore that he was sick, he abode two days still in the same place where he was. Then after that saith he to his disciples, Let us go into Judaea again. His disciples say unto him, Master, the Jews of late sought to stone thee; and goest thou thither again? Jesus answered, Are there not twelve hours in the day? If any man walk in the day, he stumbleth not, because he seeth the light of this world. But if a man walk in the night, he stumbleth, because there is no light in him. These things said he: and after that he saith unto them, Our friend Lazarus sleepeth; but I go, that I may awake him out of sleep. Then said his disciples, Lord, if he sleep, he shall do well. Howbeit Jesus spake of his death: but they thought that he had spoken of taking of rest in sleep. Then said Jesus unto them plainly, Lazarus is dead. And I am glad for your sakes that I was not there, to the intent ye may believe; nevertheless let us go unto him. Then said Thomas, which is called Didymus, unto his fellowdisciples, Let us also go, that we may die with him. Then when Jesus came, he found that he had lain in the grave four days already. Now Bethany was nigh unto Jerusalem, about fifteen furlongs off: And many of the Jews came to Martha and Mary, to comfort them concerning their brother. Then Martha, as soon as she heard that Jesus was coming, went and met him: but Mary sat still in the house. Then said Martha unto Jesus, Lord, if thou hadst been here, my brother had not died. But I know, that even now, whatsoever thou wilt ask of God, God will give it thee. Jesus saith unto her, Thy brother shall rise again. Martha saith unto him, I know that he shall rise again in the resurrection at the last day. Jesus said unto her, I am the resurrection, and the life: he that believeth in me, though he were dead, yet shall he live: And whosoever liveth and believeth in me shall never die. Believest thou this? She saith unto him, Yea, Lord: I believe that thou art the Christ, the Son of God, which should come into the world. And when she had so said, she went her way, and called Mary her sister secretly, saying, The Master is come, and calleth for thee. As soon as she heard that, she arose quickly, and came unto him. Now Jesus was not yet come into the town, but was in that place where Martha met him. The Jews then which were with her in the house, and comforted her, when they saw Mary, that she rose up hastily and went out, followed her, saying, She goeth unto the grave to weep there. Then when Mary was come where Jesus was, and saw him, she fell down at his feet, saying unto him, Lord, if thou hadst been here, my brother had not died. When Jesus therefore saw her weeping, and the Jews also weeping which came with her, he groaned in the spirit, and was troubled. And said, Where have ye laid him? They said unto him, Lord, come and see. Jesus wept. Then said the Jews, Behold how he loved him! And some of them said, Could not this man, which opened the eyes of the blind, have caused that even this man should not have died? Jesus therefore again groaning in himself cometh to the grave. It was a cave, and a stone lay upon it. Jesus said, Take ye away the stone. Martha, the sister of him that was dead, saith unto him, Lord, by this time he stinketh: for he hath been dead four days. Jesus saith unto her, Said I not unto thee, that, if thou wouldest believe, thou shouldest see the glory of God? Then they took away the stone from the place where the dead was laid. And Jesus lifted up his eyes, and said, Father, I thank thee that thou hast heard me. And I knew that thou hearest me always: but because of the people which stand by I said it, that they may believe that thou hast sent me. And when he thus had spoken, he cried with a loud voice, Lazarus, come forth. And he that was dead came forth, bound hand and foot with graveclothes: and his face was bound about with a napkin. Jesus saith unto them, Loose him, and let him go. Then many of the Jews which came to Mary, and had seen the things which Jesus did, believed on him.

❖ When Jesus got the news of Lazarus's sickness, he made a faith statement immediately, saying, "This sickness is not unto death," yet as we read the passage, we see that Lazarus died! Was Jesus lying? No, he was doing what the word tells us to do and was walking by faith and not by sight. He knew Lazarus would die; he was declaring by faith the end result of what he expected God's power to perform.

❖ Jesus purposely waited two days so Lazarus would die. In this case, the miracle was delayed for a specific purpose that God wanted to show them; however, the end result was still the same. Healing still came, even though it meant Lazarus had to be raised from the dead for it to manifest. This is one that we really need to pay attention to. This tells us there may be cases where the healing is guaranteed when we receive it by faith, but the manifestation may be delayed in presenting itself based on God's desire for a specific purpose. This is the only account of this in the gospels, and thus we see it is not common. We also see it did not mean the healing would not manifest, and it was specifically for the purpose of God getting the glory and for many to believe. This should not deter us from standing for our healing, as it will come as promised. It also should not deter us from continuing to press in daily, expecting our miracle. Again, every single account of healing except this one manifested without any delay.

❖ When Jesus knew Lazarus had died, Jesus told his disciples that they needed to go because Lazarus was asleep, and he needed to wake him. Notice how he is training us that all our words are to line up with God's truth. When the disciples were confused, Jesus had to tell them plainly that Lazarus was dead to teach them. However, this is an example to show us that when we are walking out a miracle, we don't speak doubt and death.

❖ Jesus went so far as to say that he was glad for the disciples' sake that he was not there to heal Lazarus. It was so they would believe and grow in their understanding by seeing people raised from the dead so they would be able to do it as commanded. It also shows us that God looks at the final result. He isn't all caught up in what it looks like right now.

❖ Notice how Martha responded to Jesus. She said that if he had been there, her brother would not have died (she is sharing her true anguish and upset over the situation). However, she continued with a faith statement even in the midst of terrible circumstances when she said, "But I know, that even now, whatsoever thou wilt ask of God, God will give it thee." Now, that takes faith! She was leaving the door open supernaturally for God to move.

❖ It says Jesus groaned in the spirit and wept when he saw their heartache, showing us God's compassion for what we go through during difficult times.

❖ Now, if you ever question God's willingness to heal, look at verse 37 and 38 again: "And some of them said, Could not this man, which opened the eyes of the blind, have caused that even this man should not have died? Jesus therefore again groaning in himself cometh to the grave. It was a cave, and a stone lay upon it." The people there expected Jesus to heal (and believed that he could), and Jesus groaned in himself over hearing this as it pulled at his core and the promise of the covenant. They spoke this way because they could not see what Jesus saw: that what it looked like (that was contrary to God's healing promises) was not what the end result would be.

❖ The way Jesus prayed shows us that he had prayed prior to that and believed he had received what he was expecting already. Yet he spoke the words so the others could hear it. He did not pray as though he was asking again though! He prayed as though he was thanking God. He received the miracle the very first time he prayed about it.

❖ Jesus raised Lazarus from the dead by simply calling out his name and commanding him to come forth. Now, it does say Jesus said it with a *loud voice*. I believe this was Jesus operating in total boldness as he commanded the miracle that looked so impossible to others.

I pray you have received great revelation regarding healing by reading this book. Remember, your faith comes by *continually* hearing. If you feel fear or frustration, let that be an indicator to you that you need to engage in the suggested exercises in this book. Act on the word, don't be a "hearer" only! May your health spring forth speedily!

Made in the USA
Middletown, DE
16 November 2024

64750410R00136